# A Dollar a Mile, Fifty Cents a Gate

by

## James G. Taylor, M.D.

with

## Carol J. Sanderson

NORTEX PRESS ❖ Austin, Texas

## To My Sparky

Years ago I never thought
I'd find the love I'd always sought—
God's gift was not my stumbling find;
This woman's love His rare design
Is heaped on me each day I live,
To honor her, my love to give.

*The author at the clinic, holding one of the more than 4,000 babies he delivered during his thirty-nine-year practice.*

# Contents

# Acknowledgments

Originally intended to present the people in our neck of the East Texas woods in the light I was uniquely afforded as their physician and friend, this work became more than an anecdotal memoir in the twenty-four months since Carol Sanderson and I met. Beginning with our first meeting that February night in my living room and continuing to this day, Carol draws from me voices and faces from my past by her never-ending curiosity about the era that spawned her generation. As interviewer and interviewee, our weekly meetings progressed spontaneously as Carol brought prompts that ranged from newspaper articles to music, which refreshed my recall of sights and sounds from decades past. Our collaboration at first seemed pleasantly serendipitous; however I believe that as interlopers to this region—the doctor from a small north Texas town and the writer from the largest city in the state—we developed a bond that strengthened our resolve to give our adoptive home a fair treatment, tempered by our love of the geography as much as for the character that is defined by the East Texas native. Carol's dedication to this work never wavered: Her love for poetry corresponded with my love for quotations; she leaped at the chance to research, through newspapers, library archives, and interviews with colleagues and friends, providing the bibliographical substance necessary to complete settings, time frames, and other details she couldn't trigger otherwise in my memory of an event. Our collaboration has evolved into a mutual admiration and respect for each other that knows no boundaries, to which I owe a sincere thanks to James Stanley, the Dean of Applied Arts and Sciences at Stephen F. Austin State University, who sent her to me when I asked for his recommendation of a writer for this work.

Without a doubt, Lucy Lazarine remains one of the constants in my life and I owe her more than simple thanks for her years of service to my practice as well as her professional and moral support since my retirement.

For his unwavering support of me professionally regarding my affiliation with Memorial Hospital, I cannot say enough about its administrator, G. W. Jones. He epitomizes the concept of goodwill ambassador in his professional capacity, but it is his sincere friendship beyond that arena I most appreciate.

To my friends who encouraged me by listening to my oft-repeated refrains these past few years over coffee and cards, let this small but respectable space be my humble thanks for your patience: S. M. (Moss) Adams, Jr., Mike Allen, Guy Anderson, B. F. Ashcroft, George Clark, Jr., Campbell Cox, Arlis Hibbard, A. T. Mast, Jr., R. G. (Bob) Muckleroy, Kelso Woodward, and Tom Wright.

Ken Dorsett's passing this summer does not lessen a debt of gratitude for his generous interviews and admiration of his zest for life in general. Hopefully, these traits are reflected in the chapter on polio, which owes much to his personal experience with "a paralyzing fear."

Finally, I cannot overstate the importance to my well-being that one young man has played during the past two years. As much for physical as well as moral support I look to my stepson, John Fleming. For all the errands, the companionship when Norma had to step out, and above all, his belief and help in furthering this project, I am eternally grateful to John.

As I relinquish these stories beloved to me and my cherished circle of friends and family, I've come to realize how very restrictive the written voice is. The reader can only experience what is committed to a one-dimensional format, relying upon our choice of words to accurately relay the emotions and intellect that accompanied the setting, whether it was a psychiatric ward in Parkland or a fork in the road at Alazan. May the reader derive as much pleasure from these stories as Carol and I derived in the re-creation.

JAMES G. TAYLOR
July 15, 2000

# Introduction

## FRUITCAKES

In 1946, hoping to start a medical practice, I visited a town nationally-acclaimed for a German baker's concoction called the Original Deluxe. I was thirty-one years old, newly discharged from the service with four years of training behind me under some of the finest specialists in the country.

What attracted me to Corsicana, a farm and rail center that rose up between the high plains of North Texas and the piney-woods of East Texas a century ago, was what attracted many young men looking forward to civilian life after the war: A place where we could put down roots and become a part of a community. After certifying and patching up soldiers for duty, first at San Antonio's Aviation Cadet Center and toward the end of the war, at San Marcos Army Airfield, I wanted more than anything the chance to pursue the field for which I felt best trained— gynecology and obstetrics. More than this, which I wouldn't realize until much later, I needed the rapport with people that family practice in a small town engenders.

It didn't take me long to determine that this settlement within an hour of the metropolis of Dallas couldn't support a new physician, much less two, as my wife was eager to start a practice of her own. Queries about the need for a gynecologist and pediatrician in the sparsely-populated county met with looks ranging from mild amusement to thinly-disguised bewilderment. With our daughter Sally already a lively toddler, Sarah and I kept driving, heading for the more logical place to settle, her hometown.

Without a doubt, my wife's parents being close by to help raise Sally figured significantly in our rationale for setting up practices in Nacogdoches. When I try to single out a specific event, however, a night in December of 1942 remains the most vivid reminder of what really drew me to the oldest town in Texas.

Sarah and I were visiting her parents that Christmas, just after our first wedding anniversary. Like many who married at such a tumultuous time in American history, we'd spent most of the year apart, Sarah finishing her internship at Parkland Hospital in Dallas, while I entered the service and began my career as a doctor at an 1,100-bed hospital for a cadet training center in San Antonio. Spending the holiday with the Fergusons was as close a return to the "normal" life I'd known before the war; Sarah and I not only observed our first wedding anniversary that week, but we had a beautiful three-week-old daughter with us to introduce to the grandparents.

As I stepped out on the front porch of my in-laws' home that Saturday afternoon on December 26, I heard a roar I hadn't noticed in previous visits. I called out to Sarah's mother, "Do you often hear the train from your house?" When she answered back "Not usually," I felt a premonition of danger come over me. Invisible hairs raised on the back of my neck, because I was beginning to make a connection between the now unnatural roar, unseasonably balmy weather, and the sickly, gray-green sky.

Hurrying inside to turn on the radio, I told Sarah I thought a tornado must be close by. As we all listened to the news, a steady rain began pelting the house. Within the hour, sporadic reports of a tornado flattening the nearby communities of Appleby and Holly Springs confirmed my fears. Though the city of Nacogdoches seemed to escape the funnel cloud, reports of storm damage were coming in. Sarah and I left the Ferguson home to volunteer medical aid for City Memorial Hospital.

At the hospital, Dr. Tucker met us sporting a headlamp that would make a frog-gigger proud. Though the storm had knocked out power lines to the hospital, he assured us that the staff had the situation under control and suggested we check with the downtown fire station, where temporary first aid was being set up.

It was a busy night, but one thankfully with no casualties. The majority of the injured required broken bones to be splinted and lacerations closed. Though I think Sarah and I were the only doctors to show up at the fire station, the number of townspeople who surrounded us with offers to help made all the difference in the quality of care we provided for the stream of bedraggled storm victims coming in. From fetching supplies to holding crying children, these East Texans stood behind us every minute, treating Sarah and me as well as the injured like we were special guests in their homes, making sure we wanted for nothing. Some names were exchanged, I'm sure, but I wasn't listening as much as I was observing. I was consistently amazed by these people who responded to strangers in distress, their motivation pure and simple compassion.

What I realized years later was that the people in the fire station that night never considered each other strangers, only neighbors whose names they had not learned. Even today, this is one of the strongest traits of East Texans. More than courtesy, more than a sense of Christian duty, it's a self-confidence that the people who have lived here for several generations exude. That self-confidence gives them an air of openness and friendliness toward people in need. Among some very rural people who had no worldly goods to share, I witnessed a generosity of spirit that over the course of my thirty-nine-year practice here, confirmed my initial impression of this trait.

The stories that resulted in the chapters to follow were inspired by the spirit of these East Texans. If I achieve nothing more than to reveal the unique character of this community, the recording of these true accounts of people and events will be one of my worthier efforts. To family and friends who have encouraged me to share my experiences as a physician with the world outside of East Texas, I owe a great deal for the initial nudge that led to this book.

*Norma and James G. Taylor, Christmas 1999.*

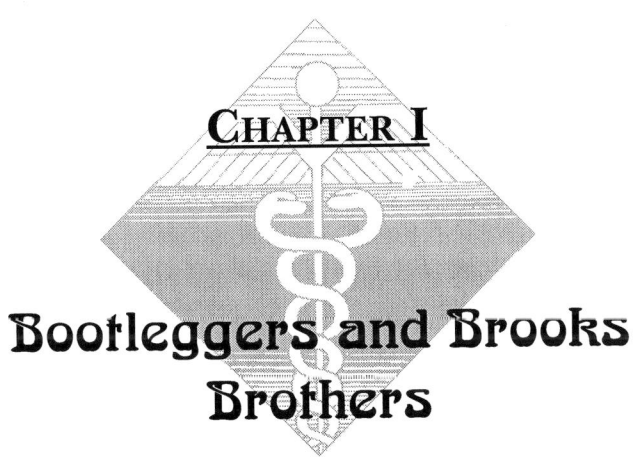

# Bootleggers and Brooks Brothers

Depending on the season, most of them were or had been farmers, loggers, or bootleggers. One humid July morning a group of East Texans huddled over dominoes at the back of Fuller's General Store while patrons came in to pick up the latest news: What was this about a new preacher coming to the Freewill Baptist Church? Rumors flew that the price of gasoline was going up. It was 1946, and the store was second only to the Chireno Post Office six miles away as a reliable trade center for gossip.

Corrugated tin cans of chili, sardines, pork and beans and the like solidly greeted customers from whitewashed plank shelving prominently displayed at the front of the store. Perishables like sweet whole milk in glass bottles and butter in one-pound cheese-clothed chunks shared refrigerated cases off to one side. An uneven floor the color of pecan hulls felt as firm as the hard-packed clay eighteen inches below it, the two-bys probably cut from rich lighter pine.

Such was the setting of my baptism into the Black Jack community on Attoyac Bayou.

I was surprised to see cars parked on either side of a single gasoline pump in a grassless area. After driving what seemed a long way in the woods and passing only one or two farmhouses, I wondered how a general store could stay in business in such isolation.

As the squeaky hinges of the loosely-hinged screened door to the entrance of the store swung behind me, I had little notion of the impact my appearance would make.

"Mornin'," a voice greeted me from behind a cash register. I nodded a return greeting and wasted no time getting to the reason for stopping there.

"I've come this far," I said to the clerk, as if he understood what the word "far" encompassed for a young doctor on one of his first housecalls in unfamiliar country. "Can you tell me where Tom Fuller lives? "

"Never heard of him," came the gruff reply. Hardly taking his eyes off me he relayed the question to the domino players, "Anybody know where Tom Fuller lives?"

I had their undivided attention, as evidenced by a chorus of "naw". To the last man there, they had never heard of Tom Fuller.

Though I doubted anyone was interested, I decided to be up front about my business there. "Well, I'm a new doctor in Nacogdoches and thought I'd better come out to see him because his wife said he had a 103 fever."

This generated a buzz and the immediate response, "Hell, why didn't you say so before? We thought you were an insurance salesman or a government man the way you was dressed."

Not realizing that my clothes would mark me as anything other than a professional, I had a lot to learn. Since my earliest days in medical school, I'd been coached about the proper dress among physicians. A coat and tie, certainly, to which I added a hat, usually tweed, which served a dual purpose: Not only did it protect my shorn head, which earned me the nickname "Kojack" during the years Telly Savalas played the popular detective on TV, but it was a perfect ice-breaker with children when I made housecalls. After I'd show them how I could flip it to land upright on my head, they were thrilled to be allowed to play with it while I saw to the patient.

After my discharge from the service, the traditional trouser-and-jacket suit was my uniform. If it was 100 degrees in the shade, I'd still make housecalls in a long-sleeved shirt with French cuffs beneath a sports coat and matching slacks I had tailored in Dallas. It went against my sense of identity to dress otherwise. To men clad in overalls and home-stitched cotton drawers—some bare-footed—such attire not only indicated that I was a stranger to their neck of the woods, but that I might be in a profession that warranted caution in their words and actions in my presence.

As I turned to leave, at least a half dozen men offered to go with me to the Fuller house. The about-face in their reception once they learned I was a doctor warmed me and I leaned forward expectantly as one of them took me aside before we were halfway to the car.

"Don't come to these parts dressed like someone from Houston or Dallas," was all he had to say but I knew I was accepted.

I am no stranger to compromise. In the years that followed, whether I made calls to Black Jack or Melrose or any one of the dozens of communities like them where the people protected one another with similar acts of bluff and cover, I left my coat in the car.

The practice was picking up. That first summer in Nacogdoches, when I wasn't seeing patients in the small office I rented over Swift Brothers and Smith Pharmacy, I took calls from home any hour and any day of the week. On a mid-June afternoon, my telephone rang.

"You that new doctor?"

"Yeah."

"How much do you charge for a country call?"

"A dollar a mile and 50 cents a gate. Twenty-five cents extra if there's a biting dog on the place."

Though I never held patients to this fee, it was a useful quote to use early in my practice, when I had difficulty weeding out those simply seeking a social call from those truly needing medical assistance.

"Well, come out to the forks of the road at Alazan. I'll meetcha and open the gate."

I had no doubt as to the seriousness of the call. I'd grown familiar with the monosyllabic delivery of men who lived and worked in an environment that offered them rare contact with people outside immediate family and neighbors.

It wasn't the first or last time I hit the road bound for a place with minimal directions and no clue as to the identity or condition of my patient. It was, however, my first visit to Alazan.

As I drove past a cemetery and a church that confirmed landmarks I had been told to watch for on the way to Alazan, I tucked road signs like Gravel Ridge and Macedonia Baptist Church in the back of my mind, hoping I could find them again in the dark if I ran late getting home.

Like most summer days in East Texas, the humidity rose with the sun. By 10:00 A.M. people indoors relied on well-placed windows for ventilation, accepting the light perspiration and limp clothes as part of the season. If they worked outside at any kind of labor, their clothes would bear the stain of sweat rich in sodium chloride. This being prior to the days of hypertension alerts and the link to salt, everyone's diet included a variety of sodium-enriched foods, from vegetables cooked with salt pork to the dependence on salt as a leavening agent in most baked goods.

On such a day, I didn't mind the pollen-choked dust that swirled in the car as I made my way down a dirt road that wound through loblolly and sweetgum. I left all the windows open in the '46 Ford Club Coupe to fully appreciate what breeze could be generated at 35 miles per hour. Like a kind of welcoming committee, the gritty wind tugged at the cotton shirt sticking to my back and armpits.

As instructed by the caller, I stopped at the fork in the road. The dust had barely settled on my hood when I was startled by a tall man in overalls stepping out of a row of sunflowers as if he'd been growing alongside them, their heads bobbing at the same height.

He slid in the passenger side of my car and directed me down what was little more than a lane, somewhat wider than a cow trail but covered with tall Bermuda grass nonetheless. Easing the Coupe across a dry creek bed, I was about to suggest we park and walk the rest of the way, when a clearing came into view that left little doubt in my mind we had reached our destination.

In a dry county, the isolation of communities like Alazan, not to mention the lack of paved roads, with farm houses scattered between by briar thickets and dense timber, presented an ideal setting for bootlegging. Men who walked the seasons behind mule-drawn plows, from the potato-planting days of February 'til the turning of the rows after autumn's pumpkin harvest, were as drawn to the profit side of bootleg whiskey as those who had no land to work. Such income made up for the inconsistent outcome of living off the land, made educating their children a manageable expense and in some cases, provided a good living as the only source of cash flow.

The patient, though prominent because of his size and supine position on a grassy knoll, was overshadowed by other elements at the site, notwithstanding a whiskey still operation. Positioned next to a spring-fed creek, two 55-gallon wooden drums competed with the patient for attention. One barrel, the cooking drum, had a small fire built beneath it, a half-emptied sack of steel-cut corn chops on the ground next to it. Copper tubing linked the cooking drum to a cooling drum a few feet away, where the vapors produced from heating 50 pounds of sugar, 50 pounds of corn chops, and 35 gallons of creek water condensed through the tubing as it snaked to a spout at the bottom of the receiving drum. There the whiskey product was collected in whatever was handy—fruit jars, ceramic jugs, or cola bottles.

A half dozen men surveyed me from strategic positions, scattered in a semi-circle at the edge of the clearing. Their wariness was as apparent as the steam rising from the copper tubing where it entered the cooling drum. I felt that something as unannounced as a sneeze from me would send them scurrying into the dark timber. Though each of them was armed, the implications of this were lost on me once I reached the patient.

His overalls accentuating his obesity, the bearded middle-aged man sweated profusely, conscious but short of breath and complaining of pains in his chest. His condition didn't leave much doubt that he was having a coronary occlusion.

After checking his blood pressure, I reached for a vial of morphine from my bag. Not only was morphine a fast-acting painkiller, it dilated the arteries. After diluting a conservative dose of the powdered drug, I gave the patient an injection to subdue the chest pain. Before long, I was relieved to see that his blood pressure, initially 180/100, had dropped considerably. Once the patient could breathe without difficulty, the atmosphere in that clearing changed accordingly, the men gathering closer around me yet relaxed and curious.

Under the watchful eyes of the bootleggers, I wrote a couple of prescriptions for the patient. Under their intimidating stares I did what any nervous man would do in unfamiliar territory; I found a stump to sit on and stopped to chat.

As I got up to leave, I advised them how to get the prescriptions filled. In the meantime, I allowed, a few sips of whiskey would help to relieve the angina pain.

In a double-edged tone, the sunflower man said "We want you to forget what you've seen out here."

"I don't know what you mean."

"That's what we mean."

I played along. "Can somebody help me back to the road. I don't know where I am."

I wasn't sure how much they trusted me until I had a call from three other bootleggers the next week for ailments ranging from strep throat to infected boils.

Before calling on bootleggers as patients, my knowledge of whiskey-making came from my father, whose advice on how to tell good homemade whiskey from bad remains with me to this day: If you shake a pint jar of homemade whiskey and bring a bead to the surface, it's okay to drink; if it doesn't bead up, it probably contains an undesirable by-product known as fusel oil, which adversely affects the liver in a relatively short period of time.

In addition to this bit of knowledge, I considered myself educated when I learned the two types of bootlegger in East Texas: Those that made their own whiskey and sold it in fruit pint jars and those that bought labels in wet counties, then sold labeled pints to buyers for a profit. On a later house call to one of these men, I was shown an impressively neat stack of five-dollar bills in a footlocker.

He ironed money he said because "wrinkled bills don't stack well."

Over the next thirty years I made many calls to Alazan that had nothing to do with bootleggers. I doubt that any cemented my welcome as much as the first call.

# CHAPTER II

# 1946: A Turning Point

"Sioux City Sue, Sioux City Sue,
Your hair is red, your eyes are blue,
I'd swap my horse and dog for you,
Sioux City Sue, Sioux City Sue,
There ain't no gal as true
As my Sioux City Sue."

A song about a Nebraska cowboy courting a girl in Iowa. In the spring of 1946, it was the most popular folk record in the country. Bing Crosby made a signature recording of it that year, Gene Autry starred in a movie under that title, and everyone I knew in Nacogdoches was singing "Sioux City Sue."

With V-J Day nearly a year behind us, it was time to get on with civilian life.

Dallas held no great lure for me. Having grown up in a largely Germanic community in North Texas and receiving the better part of my medical training at air bases near San Antonio and San Marcos, the land of cattle ranches and peach orchards between San Marcos and Brenham beckoned.

Family considerations, however, led me to East Texas.

For a young family man trying to make the leap from government service to starting from scratch in a small town, practicality pointed to Nacogdoches. Just a few months before Pearl Harbor, I'd met a brilliant medical student named Sarah Ferguson, who called Nacogdoches home. Following the disastrous events of December 7, the nation's swift reaction by declaring war on Japan influenced many of my generation to marry before we took an oath to the service and chanced transfer to the other side of the world. Consequently, Sarah and I married just after I enlisted, late that December. Like so many others, we were separated most of the war, even though I was stationed in Texas for the duration.

Earning a specialty in pediatrics, Sarah planned to practice in Nacogdoches. Her parents encouraged us to settle there, looking forward to being closer to our daughter Sally. The family connection wasn't the sole motivation for moving to the area. Due to frequent visits to Sarah's family during the war, I'd acquired a circle of friends whose children I would deliver, hands I would hold in their last hours, and who would see me through personal trauma over the next forty years.

One of our favorite forms of entertainment after the war in East Texas was square dancing. My father had few equals as a "breakdown" fiddle player and in the course of accompanying him to social gatherings in Cleburne, I listened to and mimicked square dance calling at an early age. When our friends in Nacogdoches found out I knew a few calls, they'd ask me to stand in for a few numbers. As couples scooted across the hardwood floor of the Aikman Gym on the SFA campus one night, I tried some new lyrics on them.

> "Ain't got no farm, ain't got no ranch,
> make my livin' on Eggnog Branch;
> Whoop it up, boys, everybody dance."

Of course, everyone there knew where Eggnog Branch was; by the use of the impromptu lyrics, I was hoping to impress upon those who knew me only as the new doctor in town that this was my home and I was now one of them.

Most of the men I counted on then and now matured under the shadow of the strongest country in the world being at war.

Once upon a time, we were soldiers in uniforms emblazoned with the rank of "Ensign" or "Lieutenant" or "Major." After the war, rank and uniform were traded for "Doctor," "Mr. City Attorney," and so on. Today, it's simply Jim, Moss, Guy, Adlai, Bob, Kelso, and Tom.

Most of these Nacogdoches natives were pursuing degrees at various state colleges when the war came into our lives. Between early 1942 and the middle of 1943, all of them would enlist and serve through V-J Day.

Jim.

James G. Taylor, Jr. of Cleburne, Texas. I was turned down the first time I tried to enlist, because of the critical shortage of doctors in this country and the fact that I within a few months of completing my residency at Parkland Hospital in Dallas. I wanted desperately to be a flight surgeon, a service option that was discontinued shortly before I was commissioned at San Antonio Aviation Cadet Training Center. From 1942 until 1946, I served as a medical officer, performing everything from plastic surgery to hemorrhoidectomies in San Antonio, then transferring to San Marcos Army Airfield as Chief of Surgery until the end of the war.

Moss.

S. M. Adams, Jr. passed the bar prior to Pearl Harbor, ready to join the family law firm. Instead, he took on a different family—the Navy—in 1942. Trained on the USS *Prairie State* (a sister ship to the *Maine*), Moss served on a tanker that fueled ships in the Atlantic until he could take flight training. From September, 1942 until the end of the war, he trained cadet pilots in Jacksonville, Florida.

Guy.

A native of Calvert, Texas, Guy Anderson was enrolled at the University of Texas until 1942, when he enlisted and flew missions in B-26s in the Pacific theater of war.

Adlai.

Bitten hard by the pilot bug, A. T. Mast, Jr. made the leap to military service before the U.S. entered the war, joining the British Royal Air Force while a senior at the University of Texas and returning to fly for the U.S. in 1942.

Bob.

Son of the owner of the ice cream factory in Nacogdoches,

R. G. Muckleroy studied at Stephen F. Austin State College and Texas A&M until June, 1943, when he joined the Army Veterinary Corps, where he served for the duration of the war.

Kelso.

The son of an engineer at the largest sawmill in the Nacogdoches area, Kelso Woodward joined the 32nd Infantry in 1942, later serving in the Philippines and New Guinea, ending his tour in 1946 in occupied Japan.

Tom.

A student at Stephen F. Austin State College in 1941, Tom Wright had joined the National Guard prior to Pearl Harbor. After completing Officers' Candidate School in North Carolina, he served with an antiaircraft artillery unit in both the North African and European theaters of war.

Like old knights at a white-shrouded roundtable, we meet several times a week for coffee at the hotel. We rarely talk about the war; most of us simply saw it as our duty and would rather leave it in that part of memory that's collecting dust, like an old set of encyclopedias in the attic. Over the years, media blitzes about U.S. military involvement in a Middle-eastern desert or east European village stir us to question the wisdom of intervening in conflicts that have raged for centuries; nevertheless, we voice respect for the courage of those who serve when called.

If we'd all had the ability (maybe it was really a matter of choice; I believe ability comes with practice), we would have been fliers. What eighteen-year-old didn't fantasize about strafing runs or dogfights in a Hurricane Hawker?

One Nacogdoches boy followed his fantasy.

In the spring of 1941, A. T. Mast, Jr. had finals to study for. A senior in the School of Business at the University of Texas, he'd also recently completed a civilian pilot training course, with the notion that he would enter the Navy as an ensign immediately after graduation.

A visiting RAF wing commander to the campus changed his plans. The recruiter targeted seniors who fulfilled the criteria of 250 hours flying time and passing grades, promising exemption from finals if they joined. Adlai and three others threw up their hands to volunteer.

One of sixteen Americans to train with the RAF in Mesa,

Arizona, just months before the attack on Pearl Harbor, Adlai thought he had it made at Falcon Field. The arid sunny climate offered a welcome contrast to the humid, rainy East Texas weather, and he couldn't believe that they weren't required to march. They even had a swimming pool. Best of all, they got to fly.

In a program of pursuit pilot training that gave condolences to the family rather than grades if the student failed, the RAF thrust the cadets into dogfights, formation flying, and air-to-ground gunnery. In Adlai's estimation, there was only one drawback.

"The British boys didn't like us particularly," Adlai recalls. In addition to an age gap—the Americans were generally two to four years older—the Brits had little mechanical experience among them. "Most had never driven a car." Such mechanical naiveté increased the natural rivalry between British and American cadets, especially if the Americans had been raised in East Texas running farm equipment and driving trucks since they were tall enough to see over the steering wheel.

When the attack on Pearl Harbor in December of 1941 prompted the U.S. Army Air Corps to "recall" pilots like Adlai, releasing them from service to the RAF, Adlai had to be oriented to four-engine aircraft. The instrument flying time he logged for the U.S. over the next two years combined with the RAF experience flying B24s and C24s led to a variety of assignments that took him to Iceland, North Africa, and India. Ironically, it was an incident at an American airfield near the end of the war that crippled his plane and nearly ended his career.

It began in Redding, Pennsylvania, where Adlai and his C54 crew were summoned during the blustery, miserable winter of 1945. From Redding, their orders were to fly to Billings, Montana, where they would refuel. The aircraft was yet to be seen. Even repeated warnings from a ground engineer who told them that the runway would be a little short and they'd need to take off at full throttle to get up didn't prepare them for the type of aircraft they were getting.

"When we got out to the runway, what we saw was a specially-designed plane with a Plexiglas bottom. They had cameras all over the interior. We weren't really familiar with the plane and saw all this for the first time as we headed to the cockpit [to take off]." It was a modified B-29, customized in Kodak, Pennsylvania for the purpose of taking pictures of the deployment of an atomic bomb from the belly of the plane.

True to the ground engineer's admonitions, takeoff was tricky due to the weight of the plane. "My copilot asked me where the hell we were going because we were pulling up as hard as we could but barely cleared some of the buildings in Redding." From there, the flight went without a hitch until they had to stop for refueling in Montana. The airport was small, but had two types of runways, an asphalt-type called macadam and concrete.

About seventy-five miles from the airport, Adlai requested permission from the control tower to land on the concrete runway, indicated by a facilities chart to be the longer one.

"Negatory," came the deliberately slow response. "Your instructions are to land at the following coordinates, or not at all."

Adlai was in a bind. Despite his assurance to the tower man that he would assume all responsibility for the landing, the airport employee denied his request for that runway because of a crosswind. Adlai had no choice but to land as instructed.

"As soon as I let my nosewheel down, I hit a soft spot in the runway and knocked the wheel off." Between the wind gusts, the inferior runway and the awkward weight-distribution of the plane, disaster prevailed. Though he'd slowed the plane as much as possible before losing the nosewheel, Adlai could only guide it to a grinding halt as the props and Plexiglas disintegrated against the macadam surface. "The crew was laughing and hollering because they knew this meant we weren't going to the South Pacific." Though the orders gave few details of their mission, they'd been aware of the destination. The men were war-weary. Some had been out of the country for the duration of the war and were apprehensive, to say the least, about leaving the states again.

The specter of a court martial hovering in the back of his mind, Adlai made a dreaded call to a general in Washington. "Mast, I hope you're drunk," was the general's response. When Adlai apprised him of the extent of the damage, the general told him to leave the wreckage as it was, close the field down, and post guards.

While he waited on the arrival of the nearest commanding officer, Adlai called his father in Nacogdoches.

"I've had a little hard luck," he began. "I've torn up this plane pretty badly."

His father's immediate response of "Are you gonna have to pay for it?" didn't help his morale.

Within a few hours a general from the airbase at Great Falls, Montana arrived, along with an entourage. After watching the C.O. grill Adlai and tell him he was under house arrest with a court martial pending, an intelligence officer with the entourage stepped in and gave the East Texas boy a glimmer of hope.

"Come with me to the tower," he told Adlai. The intelligence officer, a major, had the tower personnel play back a tape recording of Adlai's radio call for the landing. All such transmissions over the air were recorded by law, the major explained. As they listened to the tape, Adlai's request and the tower man's refusal played back clearly, word for word. The major put his arm around the young pilot and said, "Mast, you're saved."

The Army stood behind Adlai, based on the control tower tape and his military record. Once he was apprised of the full circumstances, the general even commended him for his landing skill against natural and man-made adversity.

I asked Adlai why he never flew after the war. He tells me he figures he's already used all the luck he was entitled to.

What he brought back to a small town in East Texas after having flown for two countries during the war was a mindset.

The pressure of being responsible for other men's lives and deaths shaped such a mindset, as well as random association with men of all colors and creeds who had sworn to do the same. No matter who they are before they leave home, men who survive a war to return are never the same as when they left. Even "home" takes on a different meaning to them.

The overall effect is a broadening of perspective. Depending on how traumatic the experience, some choose to retreat from society, to resist change. Others, like Adlai, choose to put those experiences to use, viewing change as not only necessary but healthy.

When I reflect on the time that's passed since the war years, I marvel at the chain of events that brought me to East Texas and the bond I've formed with men I hardly knew in 1946.

These men returned to Nacogdoches to be reunited with family or to marry within families already settled here. Like all families, the group that meets for coffee has seen death and new life come into our circle.

To our roundtable, the voices of Henry Schmidt and George Clark, Jr., added a reassuring reminder to the circle that no matter how many years march between us and the era of our youth, our voices—thoughts, ideals, and aspirations—find kinship once again. Sadly, their voices have been stilled. Since their passing, two more have taken their place. An Englishman who flew for the RAF and later for the U.S., Mike Allen came to Nacogdoches in recent years to be close to family. A family business induced B. F. Ashcroft to move to Nacogdoches shortly after the war, after thirty-six months of duty as a Naval watch officer in the Hawaiian Islands.

Voices from the generation succeeding us have become semi-regulars. "Youngsters" like Campbell Cox, George Clark, III, and Arlis Hibbard will no doubt carry on the coffee tradition, where e-mail and cell phones have yet to find us. Just men who sit in a circle and talk; sometimes about cattle, sometimes about the University, always about life.

# CHAPTER III

## Town and Country

"What do you want to go there for? The land's all wore out and the people all have hookworm."

This was my father's reaction when I told him I was going to start a practice in Nacogdoches. From his perspective—a man who'd spent most of his entrepreneurial life in north Texas cotton country—East Texans had little to brag about. What land wasn't covered with timber was poor, comparatively-speaking; the idea of rotating crops to enrich the soil hadn't been implemented. The red clay subsoil that criss-crossed counties between river bottoms discouraged fence-building. If there'd been no rain for a couple of weeks, the stoutest field hand couldn't penetrate it with a post-hole digger.

When the slow, soaking rains come, the same clay mutated from granite to an oil slick overnight, frustrating not only those setting posts but anyone who drives on unpaved county roads.If the road had little change in elevation, a car had a chance of staying on it. The steeper the grade, the better the chance that the driver would careen into a ditch and have to wait for assistance from a farmer with a John Deere to pull him out.

The summer we moved to East Texas, Nacogdoches County was as lush and green as I'd ever seen it. What we call a right-of-way, or shoulder, didn't exist. Where ditches hadn't been washed by rain runoff, dewberry vines, Chinese Tallow saplings, and a tall spindly flower we called a Black-eyed Susan overlapped the roads. The contrast to the Dallas landscape of skyscrapers, curb-and-gutter suburbs, and neon lights was staggering. Yet these were changes I could easily absorb and adapt to; after all, I'd been a frequent visitor to the area since marrying Sarah Ferguson. It was getting to know the people, both as patients and as friends, that stretched me as a doctor and member of a community. There are no people like East Texans.

The decade between 1940 and 1950 saw Nacogdoches nearly double in population, from 7,500 to over 12,000, including the seasonal eruption called enrollment at Stephen F. Austin State Teachers' College. This town where Sam Houston and Thomas J. Rusk once resided had a peculiar flavor, one of great pride in its founding fathers and historical sites yet one that would have withered beneath the mantle of dust that settles on things revered but left untouched, if not for the college. In the midst of nineteenth-century-style homes and churches and a town square surrounded by brick streets, the infusion of youth-oriented businesses and dwellings catering to college faculty and students gave the town a look of progress.

With one or two exceptions, doctors' offices were located upstairs over drugstores. By providing this space rent-free, owners of pharmacies hoped to gain by doctors' patients filling their prescriptions on the premises. When I wasn't making housecalls, my patients shared one such second-story waiting room with my wife's patients, over Swift Brothers and Smith Pharmacy. In spite of sharing office space, Dr. Ferguson and I saw little of each other professionally, primarily because the majority of my practice entailed housecalls, at least until I built my own clinic in 1954.

Sarah had a brilliant mind. Graduating from the University of Texas summa cum laude in chemistry, she entered Texas Medical School at Galveston at the age of nineteen. Five years later, she took her degree at Galveston and began an internship at Parkland in Dallas, where we met.

She also had the distinction of being the daughter of a Nacogdoches notable, T. E. Ferguson, whose administrative and teaching career with Stephen F. Austin State University and name-recognition was no inconsiderable boon to a budding medical practice. Familial contacts aside, with her natural ability and the fact that pediatrics was a burgeoning field, Sarah could have opened the office to a perpetual stream of clients. However, she restricted her patient load and refused hospital privileges so that she could spend time with our daughter, Sally.

In the early fifties, an office visit customarily ran from two to three dollars, plus another two dollars if lab work or an injection was indicated. I charged $35 for delivering a baby, barring complications. About half of my patients wouldn't or couldn't pay me. It didn't matter. There were no specialists. At least, those of us who had the training to support such a claim couldn't afford not to treat patients whose diagnoses ranged from gallstones to pneumonia. In this predominantly rural county covering nearly a thousand square miles, there were too few doctors. Consequently, I was a trained obstetrician and gynecologist practicing in the mode of a family physician for much of my career, my patients ranging from college athletes and debutantes to bankers and bootleggers.

Known as City Memorial Hospital until 1968, Nacogdoches Memorial began as a 28-bed facility servicing Nacogdoches and surrounding counties. During my first two decades of practice, it had grown to a 100-bed facility, supporting one emergency room, two small operating rooms, one of which was used for labor and delivery, and three floors that included a colored ward for OB patients as well as an isolation wing. Private rooms were simple, the size of a walk-in closet in some cases, with three functional pieces of furniture: a single bed, night stand, and chair. Bathrooms were few and strategically-located to serve patients of wards.

The staff consisted of one RN per shift, who directed nurses' aides and orderlies in everything from bathing patients to administering injections. Aides not only tended patients, but cleaned rooms and prepared instrument packs for surgery. In starched white uniforms, the staff bore these duties through extreme temperature changes, relying on space heaters during the coldest months, raising windows for air flow in the warmer periods.

I wanted to believe it was because I had taken my medical degree from Baylor, or perhaps because of the extraordinary training I received during the war that I was appointed Chief of Staff at City Memorial in 1948. I soon learned my credentials had little to do with it. The board had opted for a rotating Chief of Staff among all physicians with hospital privileges. More than a few physicians in the county were either preceptor-trained, indicating weak formal education and little or no real internship; others were elderly and inclined to outdated approaches. One such physician, unschooled about the forms of pain relief that had become common in obstetrics at the time, would simply tell a woman in labor to "just bear down."

Unlike today, we had no physicians assigned permanently to an emergency room shift. If the idea of rotating physicians on staff to cover this duty had been broached before my arrival, it had either been discarded or disregarded. As Chief of Staff, more efficient emergency-room coverage became a priority to me and, much to the dislike of some of the older physicians who viewed such an assignment as presumptuous on my part, I introduced the rotation method of coverage in the ER. This ensured that all physicians who had privileges at the hospital would be on call for emergency room duty nights and weekends.

After almost a decade of treating patients of different colors and creeds, first at the charity hospital in Dallas, then at military installations in San Antonio and San Marcos, I found the practice of confining the "coloreds" to separate wards backward, to say the least. Unfortunately, integrating wards would prove to be a challenge awaiting an era of less stability and adherence to the status quo, a generation removed from those of us who matured during World War II.

From his neatly-trimmed goatee to his freshly-pressed suits, Dr. R. E. Hanson was a dapper, well-educated man from Tennessee, a physician who'd earned the trust of blacks and whites alike by the time I started my practice. He also happened to be the only black physician practicing in Nacogdoches County at the time I started my practice. Despite his gentleman's manner and formal training from a respected southern medical school, this pre-integration era saw his practice restricted to housecalls, with no hospital privileges. Consequently, I inherited his patients on many occasions, when they were brought to the hospital for treatment or surgery.

One such emergency entailed admitting a black truck driver to the hospital with an injury to his abdomen. Internal bleeding indicated, I soon had him in surgery only to discover a split liver. After successful repair of the liver I consulted with Dr. Hanson, who had referred him to me. I described the type of suturing I'd implemented—an extremely risk-laden procedure without the proper training or suture material—the blood transfusions required, and subsequent restoration of peristalsis to the patient's intestinal tract. So intent was I about relaying the patient's treatment and condition to the man I assumed would be treating him upon release from the hospital that I didn't notice a few telltale signs preceding Dr. Hanson's reply.

Not that the twinkle in his eye seemed out of place, or the corners of his mouth lifting slowly any different than the patience-of-Job smile that was as natural to him as blinking.

"What do you think now, Dr. Hanson?" I prompted him, signifying the end of my rather self-congratulatory report.

In that dulcet, southern accent he began, "Ah think . . ."

He paused for emphasis, no doubt.

"Ah think, Dr. Taylor, that Ah'll make you a gift of that patient."

The poverty of the county was inescapable. Surgeries were performed at rural residences, with the attending physician standing flat-footed on the ground while bending over a patient placed on a makeshift table—often a waist-high front porch— usually because the patient had neither the money nor the transportation to seek help for a medical condition before it reached a critical state, requiring immediate action.

A housecall to one residence in Woden stands out in my mind even today. I had been called to check on a middle-aged woman who lived in a house that was no more than a shack, devoid of electricity and plumbing.

Shortly after my arrival, the woman I had come to examine said, "Excuse me" and without further comment, lifted her dress, pushed aside a board in the uneven flooring, and urinated through the hole exposed by the opening. As she squatted, it occurred to me that she probably thought the pneumonia I was treating her for could be dealt with in the same way she dealt with the lack of indoor plumbing. Despite the fact that penicillin was cheap and accessible by this time, she went about her day with as little thought for treating the pain from taking a deep breath as she did the inconvenience of pushing aside a board in the floor to void. Part of this approach to sickness was ignorance of the seriousness of her condition. But another part, probably even more influential, was the worry of how she would pay for a doctor's visit, much less treatment or medication.

Treating people in such living conditions haunted me at times, particularly in overcoming disease and premature deaths. My contact with two middle-aged sisters in the Woden community helped dispel the sense of despair I sometimes felt for people greatly isolated by their living circumstances.

Spinsters Sadie and Sue had never traveled beyond a mile or two of their home. As I came to know them through housecalls in the community, I noticed that they took the greatest pleasure from sights, sounds and tastes I took for granted. Accordingly, I made it a point to stop at the drugstore for a half-gallon of ice cream if I knew I had a call out that way. I thought nothing could eclipse the delight such a treat produced from them.

I was wrong.

One day in late December, I had a call to make in Etoile. On the way, I stopped by the sisters' place with some ice cream. They asked me how everything was up in Nacogdoches.

I said, "They're all decorated up for Christmas. It's pretty."

"Oh? We've never seen that."

"Sure enough?" Of course, I thought they meant they'd never seen Nacogdoches during the Christmas season. "When I come back y'all get in the car and I'll take you down and show it to you."

It was close to dark by the time I finished my calls. I pulled up to the house, halfway expecting one of the sisters to come out and tell me they didn't think I was serious about the ride to town. To my surprise, they were watching for me and didn't wait for me to kill the motor. Before I could open a door, they were climbing into the back seat of the Ford Coupe, which by today's standards, could swallow half a football team.

People in the country didn't decorate with lights as they do now, for a variety of reasons. Mostly businesses put up lights or decorated windows during the season, and these were located near the middle of town.

As we came down Orton Hill toward Main Street, one of them exclaimed, "Oh Sue, look! There's a purple one—and look at the picture of Santa in red and white! My goodness, and look at the *green* lights!"

They were seeing strings of Christmas lights for the first time, totally mesmerized by the colors brought forth at night. Neon signs delighted them as much as the holiday lights.

In their lifespan, we had fought a World War, discovered a vaccine for polio, and seen the birth and demise of the Studebaker. It was unfathomable to me that the only lumens they'd ever seen came from standard white lamp bulbs in the few fixtures in their home, and passing headlights of vehicles. For the entire tour that night, they chattered to each other as though they might be struck mute tomorrow. I think they were half afraid if they didn't say something about everything they saw, it might turn out to be a dream.

In spite of the long hours at the hospital, the cramped office space, the heartbreaking evidence of poverty in town and country, seasons that were predominantly wet, whether from humidity or fronts dropping monsoon-proportion rainfall, patients who called at my back door at all hours, a high percentage of housecalls being on log-truck rutted roads, I developed the unshakable notion that this was a different country, that there is no where else like it in Texas, and that it is as fascinating in the ways of its people as it is scenic with its red clay lanes meandering through evergreen forests. From this notion grew a bond with the land and people that I have never felt elsewhere.

And so my practice began, just a few counties away from the arenas where I'd received the best medical training Texas had to offer, with housecalls in town and country, plus office care for those who could climb the stairs.

# Chapter IV

# A Spanking Bay

My fascination with cars began with the one I built as a teenager in Denton.

My father had invested in a flour mill, where I worked when I wasn't in school. That job introduced me to two very important influences at that stage of my life: Manual labor and Bert Lansing.

Bert was a foreman at the mill. He was probably good at what he did, which was making sure that the machinery ran; I wasn't knowledgeable in those matters at the time and the years since may have dimmed my memory of that aspect. However, one thing about Bert remains vivid: He was the crudest man I ever knew.

To a teenage boy, especially raised among three sisters and my very genteel mother, this was a new and exciting experience. I didn't particularly like Bert; at times I found his language and appearance fairly disgusting. He shaved every day but had the kind of five-o'clock shadow that made his face look sooty. His hands epitomized those of a grease monkey, his palms resembling two split ham hocks that had been rolled in the dirt, his fingernails thick and uneven, storing years of oil and grit that no amount of Lava soap could budge.

My father had purchased a panel truck for use at the mill, but as Bert was pretty indispensable, he let his foreman take the truck home every night. A bachelor who was always on the

22

prowl, Bert kept a mattress in the back of that truck, in case he got lucky. As I tagged along with him on various jobs at the mill, I found Bert as fascinating as a poker game behind a tent revival. One day, as I helped him sack shorts and bran at the mill, we talked about cars.

Maybe he was trying to impress me. After all, I was the boss's son. More likely, he felt sorry for me.

"I know where you can get a DeSoto for fifty dollars," he said.

My mouth went dry at the prospect. I had about that much saved up and I knew this was the best chance I had at getting a car of my own.

"When do we go?" was all I had to say to galvanize Bert.

As soon as we could get away from the mill, we climbed into the panel truck Bert took home every night and rode a few miles west of Denton, where the DeSoto's owner lived.

Nothing could have prepared me for the shell of a DeSoto jacked up on a stump in a rural wooded grove. The owner had converted the motor to a wood-cutting device, replacing one of the rear wheels with one much smaller in diameter, which in turn operated a pulley attached to a big-toothed circular saw. All he had to do was turn the key. As the motor rumbled to life, the wheel turned, starting the saw and he slid a rough log down a makeshift table to split it.

Never mind that most of the DeSoto's body had been removed—only the hood and windshield remained; I thought it was the finest set of wheels I could buy for the money. I paid the man fifty dollars, and with Bert's help, I rescued that DeSoto from its forest grave.

Where doors and a trunk had once been, we nailed up salvaged tin and painted it blue and silver. The same salvage yard yielded a bench seat that we bolted to a refurbished floorboard. One of my sisters came up with a name for it: Little Eva, for the literary character who could jump puddles.

I took that car to college at North Texas, where it stood out for more than its appearance. The horn I rigged up in it sounded like a train whistle. As I drove to class, I'd blow the horn about a block away from the administration building. Like factory workers waiting for a shift to change, students came to associate the shrill signal of my entrance on campus every morning with the beginning of classes.

It wasn't long before I was called to the Dean's office.

Since I'd heard that he wasn't exactly pleased about my unorthodox transportation, it was no surprise when he told me to "get that paraphernalia off campus." For the rest of the time I owned the DeSoto, I parked off campus. And though I enjoyed a certain reputation with such a vehicle, I eventually sold it to the son of the president of the Women's College. The price: Fifty dollars.

A lot of other firsts occurred after that day in 1932 when I acquired the DeSoto. None had quite the impact on me as owning my first car.

It was only fitting that my practice in Nacogdoches began from the trunk of a 1946 Ford Coupe.

A blood pressure cuff and doctor's bag accompanied me everywhere. I still have the custom-made leather bag into which I crammed powders and injectible serums for emergencies that might range from heart attacks to fever convulsions. Glass syringes, a couple of 22-gauge needles, thermometer, a roll of gauze, tape and tongue depressors rounded out the bag's contents. Housecalls had me crisscrossing the county through woods and creek bottoms but included patients within the city limits as well, simply because they had no way to get to a doctor's office when they needed attention.

At the height of my private practice in East Texas, I traded vehicles almost annually for the fastest, most powerful model I could find. I wasn't drawn so much to one particular style or make as I was to what was under the hood. Between 1946 and 1954, I tested the mettle of Ford, Cadillac, and Oldsmobile.

I caught a lot of heat from friends for what they saw as extravagance on my part. If the new car was lacking in the necessary accouterments, I would locate a mechanic friend to upgrade the car with items like aluminum headers, twin-barrel carburetors, or heavy duty shock absorbers. My Dad taught me the importance of proper exhaust from an engine. This made the motor not only more powerful but more efficient. My priorities were speed and power in a stylish package but it was imperative that these coincide with an engine that didn't guzzle gasoline or clatter. Considering that the nature of many housecalls I made required a timely response, particularly when the destination was via those red corduroy roads, I found such priorities in my transportation justified.

When I had the chance to purchase a "police special" Oldsmobile in the fifties, I jumped on it. This model came with seat belts, unheard of in Nacogdoches at that time. Not that they were particularly desirable to me—I just sat on them. Because of this, I suppose, and my driving habits, some of the locals nicknamed me "Parnelli" after Parnelli Jones, a stock car racer of that era.

It didn't take me long to realize that I needed a good friend or two in the business of auto service and repair.

At a service station on North Street, I found one such good friend in John Woods. On an icy day in the fall of '46 I slid into John Woods' station, looking for someone to install chains I'd just bought to help with traction.

This was the first of many years I came to depend on John for everything from adjusting my brakes to installing a switch on my dash for the "Columbia" rear end on that Ford coupe. The Ford dealership was happy to comply with my request for this special rear end but I wanted an alteration they couldn't provide—to be able to go into overdrive at any gear at the flick of a switch. I have John to thank for this as well as several other successful alterations.

Another mechanic I came to depend on for his ingenuity worked at the Ford dealership. I believe Rayburn Parrott had no equal when it came to diagnosing a problem and improvising to achieve the optimum solution. On that red '46 Ford he put a Mallory ignition, which amounted to a hot coil, twin points, an overhead cam, and the Columbia rear end. To be able to go into overdrive in second gear really made that V-8 unwind. So skilled was he at modifying engines for maximum performance that his reputation spread well beyond East Texas.

Whenever a certain young couple drove up from Louisiana to get a tune-up for their Ford V-8, Rayburn accommodated them several times before he realized who they were. Whether it was because of an ultimatum from his boss or just that Rayburn didn't agree with their lifestyle, I never heard, but as their notoriety spread, he became "too busy" to service the car that Bonnie Parker and Clyde Barrow had been bringing to him.

Conversely, his expertise drew the law to him. While I was in the dealership one day, an FBI man came in with the complaint that his car was sluggish. The driver gave the mechanic free rein to do whatever was needed on that car. I have no doubt that the FBI agent could outrun anything on the road when he left.

Probably no one understood the power cars wielded over me better than A. J. Marshall. An engineer by profession, A. J. tinkered a great deal in his own garage. When I chanced upon a sharp little Thunderbird convertible, A. J. was the man I went to for some help with modifications. Though the T-bird came with a 312 engine, I could tell that it didn't have the response I'd grown accustomed to in the larger models I'd been driving. A. J. suggested dropping in a 289 engine with a dual exhaust. Over the course of many late nights in his garage, I handed him the wrenches while he changed out the engine.

The convertible now responded with zip. All it lacked was the roar. We put "cherry bomb" mufflers on it and for awhile, I knew no better thrill than taking the T-bird out for a spin. My son, a teenager at the time, talked me into replacing the mufflers with a more "sedate" exhaust system, because the notoriety I was getting from the noise it raised in our neighborhood embarrassed him. I ended up making that car a gift to him when he left for college.

Frequently I made in excess of fourteen housecalls a day, with one or two of these being fifteen to twenty miles out in the country. I rarely checked the speedometer. One day the Chief of Police pulled me over.

"Dr. Taylor, did you know that you're speeding?"

"Sure enough?" I grabbed the list of names I had to visit that day and offered it to him. "Look at how many calls I've got to make."

Chief M. C. Roebuck, not easily impressed or distracted by excuses of people he pulled over, whistled. "Hell, why didn't you say something before. Follow me." Still irritated that I was being delayed, I reluctantly left my car. When we got to his vehicle, he reached inside the dash and gave me a deputy's badge.

"You carry that with you and if you ever get stopped in

Nacogdoches County, use it to show 'em that you're on official business."

I never did pull the badge out but I carried it with me as long as I was in practice. Truthfully, I never needed it after that day. Everybody—especially the police—knew my car and usually waved me on. This just about ruined my driving.

After I blew the engine in my '49 Ford, I decided to try an Oldsmobile. Some of my mechanic friends claimed certain models sported an engine comparable to a rocket booster.

Returning to Nacogdoches from Douglass at about 2:00 A.M. one morning I felt the need to test the aluminum headers on my '54 Oldsmobile. Before I topped Hayter Hill, I saw the needle pass 100 mph. The headers sounded just fine. With such performance, I found it a sound practice to add a simple modification: I loaded two fifty-pound sacks of oyster shells in the trunk, which added great stability to the rear end. This was particularly effective when taking 40-degree turns on some of the rougher roads.

Several years after I traded in the Olds, I was driving in for my regular shift at the hospital when some college boys pulled up next to me at a light on North Street. Their Chevrolet Super Sport with its shiny metallic blue finish looked fast. I could tell that it was souped up from the sound of the tappets under the hood. The driver gave me the nod and revved the engine.

I was driving a Ford that year, rather unspectacular in appearance next to the Chevy. It came with an eight-track tape player and a Henry Mancini tape. It also came with a 7-liter, 428-horsepower engine, another "special" I had been lucky to get through the dealership.

When the light turned, I had no problem leaving them behind. At the next light, they weren't to be outdone. This time, tires squealed to beat hell as the Chevy tried to overtake the 7-liter. Again, they lost.

The students suffered the additional indignity of being stopped by one of Nacogdoches' finest. I recognized the officer and drove on to the hospital. The next time I saw him, I started to explain the race. The officer interrupted me.

"That's okay, Doc. I didn't give those boys a ticket. But I did give 'em a good talkin' to and told 'em never to interfere with a doctor on an emergency call again."

My conscience got the best of me. I bought seat belts for the police department that year.

During the years I practiced medicine from my car, I learned three basics about driving in East Texas.

First, if you're bald, don't drive a convertible with the top down after dark. I was tooling down a county road one mild moonlit evening, having removed the canvas top of my Cadillac convertible. My mind was probably in Tahiti or somewhere that promotes daydreams of a tranquil nature. Suddenly, a sound that strikes terror in small rodents gave me about five seconds' warning, enough to literally save my scalp.

With a great whoosh of air against his powerful wingspread, an owl swooped over me, his talons just centimeters from the top of my bare head. Luckily, I ducked just as he passed over me, but was chilled to the bone by the shadow that crossed my dash. Though wearing a hat probably would have prevented such an episode from ever happening, I always replaced the top on the convertible whenever I anticipated driving home after sunset.

The second rule of driving in East Texas is never let your gas gauge go below the halfway mark before you start hunting a gasoline pump. This is not as imperative today as it was in the fifties, with the proliferation of convenience stores, even in communities like Black Jack and Alazan. Nevertheless, a lot of these pumps are closed on Sundays.

Finally, use your brights when driving country roads after dark. The first time I drove home from Woden after a housecall in the middle of the night and realized that the black shapes in the ditch weren't moonlit shadows of shrubbery but cows, I invested in a spotlight which I had specially mounted on my car. Not only did this keep me more alert, but it gave the livestock fair warning as well. I guess the game warden knew that no poacher would drive something that made as much noise as my car. At any rate, no one ever stopped me for "spotlighting" in Nacogdoches County.

Some years after I retired, my second wife, Norma, found a framed quotation that summed up my relationship with cars. I'd forgotten about it after packing it away with other mementos in the move after Sarah died. Colonel McKewen, my C.O. in San Marcos during my service there in the forties, had a copy of it hanging in his office and when I left the Army, he sent it to me. An officer, a gentleman, and a physician who served in both world wars, he understood as well as anyone the value in choosing the right mode of travel.

I wish I could give credit to the author, but no evidence of a source appears on my thin, yellowed copy—only an artist's rendering of a nineteenth-century physician in a horsedrawn buggy and the following:

> "Today I purchased the handsomest spanking bay I could find in these parts. For in view of the human frailty to judge by appearances, it behooves a physician who wishes himself well regarded to make his rounds in a rig befitting his station."

# CHAPTER V

# The Go-Between

To my knowledge, I was the first in my family to seek the medical profession. "Why do you want to be a doctor?" my father remarked when I told him I wanted to study medicine. "If you're not worth a damn you'll starve to death and if you're worth a damn they'll kill you."

Even before I came to East Texas to open a practice that put me on call twenty-four hours a day, I had an experience that almost validated Dad's assessment of a physician's life.

How I came to face an angry, rifle-toting father in the middle of the night outside a pediatric hospital in Dallas can be summed up with two words: Bud Dryden.

When I entered medical school, I was assigned to room with another student. My father was having a good year and dropped me off at the fraternal dorm in his Chrysler Airflow. One of the young men who saw me get out was my future roommate. As I carried my bags to the room, the fair-haired "kid," slightly shorter than me but lean and fit, followed me wordlessly until we got inside the room.

His walk told me he thought he was the stud goose. His sarcastic greeting reinforced this impression. "Well, I guess you think you're somethin'." I didn't know if he referred to the car my father drove, the way I handled my luggage, or the cut of my suit.

Though I didn't like his tone I didn't want to provoke him. Not on the first day.

"I'm Jim Taylor," I said and stuck out my hand.

He took it in a grip I guess he thought would make me wince and gruffly introduced himself as Bud Dryden. As soon as I could, I let go. Striving to ignore him, I started unpacking.

This irked him. "I was an all-state blocking back at ACC," he informed me.

This was getting old, I decided. "Dryden, that doesn't impress me a damn bit."

That was all he needed. "I don't room with someone who won't fight," he growled before he jumped on me. I barely heard, "Let's see what you're made of," before we were throwing fists. I never enjoyed the physical side of confrontation but I never ran from it either. We knocked each other into our bunks, scuffling until finally, I got a hold on him he couldn't break.

"Seen enough?" I panted, hoping I sounded more cocky than I felt.

From that day on, Bud and I became lifelong friends. After this auspicious "meeting," Bud dubbed me "Tiger," a nickname I carried throughout med school and one he and his wife still use for me.

Bud was a live wire. He always said what he thought, oblivious to the consequences. On more than one occasion, I acted as a go-between. Whether it was out of a sense of loyalty to my roommate or some misguided notion that I was the only thing between Bud and impending disaster, I can't say. On reflection, I can say that my actions on his behalf were at times as impulsive and irrational as his. All he had to say was "You gonna take that from him, Tig?" to launch me into an action I often regretted.

A friendship fired in the kiln of confrontation. I know of no other way to explain the .45 pistol I held in my hand the night I confronted the man that was coming for Bud.

We'd been assigned weekend duty shifts at the Bradford Memorial Building, a pediatrics branch of Parkland Hospital. A young Mexican brought in his two-year-old daughter, dehydrated and limp from a high fever. Because of the prevalence of polio in those days, one of the first things we looked for was a stiff neck. With one hand easing her head upward off the emergency room gurney, I tried to hide my concern from her father as it became evident that her neck remained rigid when I raised her slowly to a 45 degree angle. Awake but delirious, she drifted between pain and unconsciousness. I lowered her gently back down and looked at Bud as we mouthed the same words: Spinal tap.

In a jumbled exchange of English and Spanish, we talked the father into allowing us to draw some spinal fluid. In 1940, this was a common procedure where polio or meningitis was suspected. After administering a local anesthesia, Bud inserted a needle at the base of her spine.

Even as a senior-year medical student, Bud exhibited a confidence that made the procedure look easy. The father, watching from a few feet away, never took his eyes off Bud.

Though two nurses were attending, I was probably the only person that noticed how intently the man studied the young intern bending over his gravely-ill daughter.

While I stayed with the family, Bud took the vital fluid to the lab. A vivacious young woman who had been a victim of polio as a child and wore a leg brace took the sample from him. If there can be a good side to such an impairment, I think it would be that, in her case, her handicap made her more determined than average. She performed tests with great efficiency and accuracy, obtaining the results on our patient's sample within the hour.

When Bud returned, I knew by his expression that the news was bad. In his typical no-holds-barred fashion, Bud made a pronouncement that confirmed our earlier suspicions, but failed to enlighten the Mexican father.

"No doubt about it: This child's got tubercular meningitis. There's nothing we can do for her."

To put it simply, the toddler had a fatal infection of the spinal column; though there are drugs today that would attenuate the symptoms, I'm not sure that she would have survived, given her condition when admitted. At that time, what we had been taught about the virulence of meningitis gave little room for hope. What we had been taught about those of Latin American descent banished that trace of hope. According to one of our professors at the tubercular ward in Parkland Hospital, those of Latin American blood were at a disadvantage with tuberculosis because they had no "racial immunity" in their genetic background. In other words, because of geography and the lack of exposure to this and many diseases over hundreds of years, when Hispanics came in contact with certain diseases like tuberculosis they not only had a good chance of contracting it but lacked the antibody-creating mechanism that had evolved among other peoples.

I'm not sure how we finally got the father to understand that his daughter was dying. I suppose he thought that somehow because he had brought her to a hospital something could be done and that in spite of what we said, she would make it.

Within the next twenty-four hours, she died, and invariably, the father made a connection between Bud pulling a needle from her spine and her now lifeless form. Before the sheet was drawn over her, the father went up to Bud and said, "You kill my baby, I kill you."

In as tender a way as he knew Bud replied simply, "I'm sorry."

With nothing further to offer the distraught father, Bud left the ward to go down to the basement, where interns and students bedded down between shifts. I followed him down and standing at the end of the hospital bed he'd already flopped on, I voiced my concern.

"Bud," I said, "that guy meant what he said. He's going to come after you. We'd better do something."

A master of false bravado, Bud shrugged. "Aw hell, he's not gonna bother anybody."

"Sure enough?" I said sarcastically, to no avail.

Bud remained impassive, a strange state to observe in him. "Where's that .45 your Daddy gave you when you came to Dallas?" I said, hoping to get a familiar spark from him. Muttering, "over there in the drawer," he pulled a pillow over his head, figuring if he didn't listen to me, I'd eventually go away.

Without looking back, I picked up the pistol and struck out for the park that separated the hospital from the neighborhood where the Mexican lived. It was around midnight, a clear, cool night—the kind that makes you hear things before they happen.

Just me, some trees that were planted long before Bradford Memorial was built, and the .45. "What am I doing here?" I almost said aloud. I wasn't alone for long. My fears were realized as I spotted the Mexican taking long strides across the park with a rifle in hand. Standing behind one of the gnarled, thick trees, I called out to him in the dark.

"Hernandez. I'm Dr. Taylor. You can't see me but stop and listen. Let me tell you why your baby died. Please listen to me."

I had his attention.

As I tried to explain the disease to him, he interrupted me, saying he didn't care, he had to go.

There were no other men in that hospital that night, no orderlies, no personnel other than a few night nurses. Just Bud sleeping in the basement.

As the Mexican started to advance, his desperation must have spilled out into that night air and infected me. I told him to stop.

"If you take another step," I warned him in the deepest voice I could muster, "I'm gonna shoot. This is not Dr. Dryden's fault. You go back and talk to your priest about this and have him come and talk to us."

The words slowed him but didn't make him halt. "If you come any further," I almost choked on my next words, "I'll have to kill you."

I knew I couldn't do it, though I was ready to shoot him in the leg if necessary. There was no doubt in my mind that he could shoot up the whole hospital because of the state he was in.

I don't know if he ever saw the .45 in my hands but he must have believed me because I didn't have to say anything else. He turned around and walked back the way he came.

When I got back to the hospital, I had to go down and tell Bud how close he'd come to meeting the Mexican's idea of justice. He laughed it off. Not until our friendship had been tested several more times over the years did I realize that this was his way of dealing with intense situations. When I least expected it, Bud would find a way to thank me. His gifts were sometimes unconventional, but nevertheless a form of gratitude I knew he didn't share with anyone else during the formative years of our friendship.

Before he called me about a favor one day in 1946, I hadn't seen Alfred Earl White since we muddied team jerseys on the high school football field. We'd been chums since grade school in Cleburne but our friendship was probably sealed the day we went hunting together on Nolan Creek.

Sporting our .410 shotguns, we spotted a duck at about the same time and fired, one right after the other. As if it was our next meal, we fished our prize out of the creek, anxious to show the folks what great providers we were.

On the way home, we argued over whose shot killed the duck. "I got him!" "The hell you did!" Two adolescent boys shouting at one another over one bedraggled duck presented a different picture than what we intended, I'm sure.

At any rate, when we arrived at Earl's house, we decided to settle on his mother's opinion about whose trophy it was.

"Mammy," Earl started, "Jimmie says he killed our duck. I know damn well I did."

Earl's mother immediately recognized the significance of her response on this occasion. The fact that her son said "our duck" told her he knew what really mattered; she'd address his lack of manners—the use of profanity—later.

"We'll have "our duck" for dinner if Jimmie will stay," was all she said, and while we went out to throw a ball, she cleaned and cooked that duck.

By the time we came in to eat, it didn't matter whose shot killed the duck. We both got a drumstick.

Earl went on to law school, I went to medical school, and while I was practicing medicine on young air force cadets, he was working his way up in the ranks of the Federal Bureau of Investigation. By the time I started my practice in Nacogdoches, he was stationed in Tyler, directing agents all over East Texas.

The call from Earl in 1946 involved a deserter.

"You know folks in those woods around Nacogdoches," he began. "How about going with me to pick up a deserter. They say he's living with relatives in the Etoile area."

The deserter was a draftee who had served one year before returning home.

That Earl asked me to go with him told me he had some inkling of the kind of reception a lone FBI agent might receive if he suddenly appeared in Etoile with a warrant for the young man. The average inhabitant would likely "shoot first, ask questions later" when approached by a stranger, especially if that stranger posed a threat to his way of life.

It didn't take many housecalls to the more isolated communities to discover they harbored people of a suspicious bent toward strangers appearing suddenly in their midst.

Of the different, a clan on a branch of the Attoyac had a patent. After attending one of the children in the community— an unfortunate soul who'd been born with multiple birth defects, the boy's father admitted in casual conversation that he had married his first cousin because "there weren't any others to marry out here." Within the same family, one child might rival a professional wrestler in physical strength while lack of mental acuity reduced him to little more than a fixture in a tire swing in front of the house most of his life while another child might be frail and tubercular but approaching the genius level in mathematical ability. These were of the species my friend Earl the FBI agent might have observed simply driving through rural East Texas, whether he stopped to ask directions or purchase produce.

The more dangerous type had probably eluded him, even if they weren't aware of his connection with the law. This is the species who, when they felt they could trust you, would drive down treacherous roads in the middle of a well-digger-cold night to render aid in the form of a generous dose of corn whiskey and a ride home should your car be high-centered in a ditch. People who, when it came to putting their health or their children's in your hands, would show you the old trunk where they stored five-dollar bills. With no kin in the area or a word-of-mouth recommendation from one of their own, Earl would need to watch his back in the vicinity of people who had little regard for his point of view and a livelihood to lose at his discretion.

Which family was involved, I asked him. The name he gave me over the phone was one I knew.

"Let me go down there alone," I suggested. "They're decent folks—I'll talk to your man and call you back."

Earl didn't have to express his gratitude. His quick assent to this plan conveyed more than any thanks.

A trip to Etoile was like any other drive into the woods. When it didn't rain, roads were hard washboard-rutted clay until you got near creek or river bottoms, where silty sand took over.

You could tell how well-traveled a road was by the coat of dust that accumulated on the privet shrub, muscadine vine, and poke salad that sprouted within the ditches. Houses were modest and clustered near churches and schools.

In close communities, one visit from a doctor usually was enough to educate everyone over the age of ten as to what year, make and model car the doctor drove. Once you left paved roads, which were limited to a few county roads and state highways, the other vehicular traffic dropped substantially. You might pass four cars in one day.

The deserter was there with the family when I drove up. Whether I was on a house call or just visiting, the greeting from most folks was the same: How's it goin', Doc? How about some coffee? This family was no less friendly.

When I explained what I was there for, the young man immediately confirmed that he had left his post without permission. From his point of view, as well as his family's, it was simply a case of homesickness that he gave in to at the wrong time and it—or the government—had caught up with him.

Before I left, the deserter assured me that he understood the trouble he was in and promised that he would return at once to his Army base. I had no reason to believe he wouldn't keep his word, though I doubt that he had a clue as to the gravity of his situation from the Army's point of view.

When I called Earl to relay the deserter's promise, I felt a sense of relief—the same sort of relief that usually came with seeing patients respond to treatment. Within the week Earl called to say that the deserter had returned to his outfit the following day. I never found out what his punishment was. To that particular East Texan, I suspect the reunion with his family and place was worth the consequences.

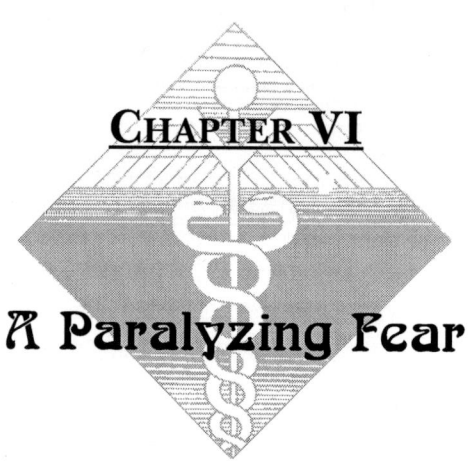

# CHAPTER VI

# A Paralyzing Fear

"I was ten or twelve years old, attending school at the Mound Street campus, which housed all grades at the time. Mother was working and couldn't take me so she trusted me to walk downtown to Dr. Henry's office after school to get the shot. I dreaded going up those steps—dark and wooden and they creaked—and guys with their tobacco cans everywhere. Halfway up you could hear the syringes boiling, rattling against a beaker. Before disposables, glass syringes and hypodermic needles were sterilized on burners in the doctor's office. I knew that sound because I had seen my mother, an R.N., sterilizing syringes and needles on the stove. I also knew enough to be afraid of getting polio from the shot."

Norma Fleming Taylor


The summer of 1952 started out like any other. Screened doors twanged from the sound of June bugs slapping against them on muggy nights. During the day, temperatures soared into the nineties. School doors closed for summer and Nacogdoches youth dotted the streets on Schwinn bicycles, younger ones pedaling furiously to produce that unique clickety-clack made by playing cards clothespinned to their spokes. Adolescent boys and tom-boyish girls raced to the corner grocery to fan through the latest comic books and buy all-day suckers or a bottle of Delaware Punch. Teenage girls met at the tennis court, teenage boys at the ballpark. And children of all ages congregated at the city swimming pool, now part of the Stephen F. Austin State University campus.

Before air-conditioned homes and recreation centers, swimming was probably the premier summer activity of kids growing up in East Texas. Those growing up outside the city climbed elms and water oaks to tie thick cotton rope around low-slung limbs so they could swing Tarzan-like over Carrizo Creek or Loco Bayou. Remnants of those rope swings today on trees that have survived disease, flood, and the lumber demand are witness to thirty-plus summers of farmers' sons and daughters squealing as they dropped into the silt-stirred water.

That summer, the innocence of such activity was forever marred by the diagnosis of four cases of polio in the county in a single week.

Poliomyelitis. At the turn of the century, the disease was commonly referred to as infantile paralysis. A popular medical reference published in 1905, *Medicology, or Home Encyclopedia of Health* defined infantile paralysis as "a variety [of nervous disease] developed in young children and occasionally present from time of birth. As a rule this palsy arises from disease of the spinal cord and its membranes." Treatment, according to this guide for the lay person, concentrated on "preventing complete loss of power by persevering and systematic movements, application of galvanism and exercise as suggested in the article on hemiplegia."

If the disease had not struck a certain thirty-nine-year-old man in the summer of 1921, I doubt the fifties would have seen the leaders it did in the quest for a vaccine. His political career just taking off with a successful stint as state senator and assistant secretary of the Navy, Franklin D. Roosevelt's star could well have fallen had it not been for his determination to succeed in spite of the paralysis that robbed him overnight of the use of his legs. Sometime after he entered the White House, FDR was asked how he coped with the strain of political life. His reply "If you had spent two years in bed trying to wiggle your toe, after that anything would seem easy" illustrates the positive attitude that factored into his popularity with working-class people. The wealthy, privileged Roosevelt established a rapport with the average American based on action as well as words, championing much-needed research, treatment, and education about polio.

Fundraising for research began with White House balls in the thirties, followed by the creation of the March of Dimes, a phrase coined from a popular newsreel titled "March of Time." Not only did the March of Dimes enlist celebrities such as Mickey Rooney, Lucille Ball, and Rock Hudson for fundraising, but it initiated such programs as the "porch lights" donations, a campaign successfully adopted by the Mothers' March of Dimes in Nacogdoches. This campaign sent volunteers to homes where porch lights were left on between 7:00 and 8:00 P.M. to signify that donations could be collected from them. Though the funds raised for March of Dimes target a multitude of birth defects today, with polio victims constituting a minority, Nacogdoches volunteers still canvas their neighbors during this unique holdover of the porch light days. If a survey was initiated, I believe it would find a high percentage of these local volunteers to be survivors of polio or related to someone whose life was immeasurably altered by it.

Between 1905 and 1952, the definition of the disease didn't change. Thanks to Franklin D. Roosevelt in the thirties, the public's awareness did. And thanks to Jonas Salk in the fifties, prevention through vaccination became a reality. In 1916, when the first real epidemic of this century occurred, New York City responded by washing down city streets and killing thousands of stray cats, thought to be carriers of infantile paralysis. In 1952, control measures such as avoidance of communal swimming and tonsillectomies during periods of increased incidence reflected the medical community's lack of progress in pinpointing the cause. We still didn't know why it struck some and not others. I suspect that a lot of kids contracted it in the mildest form, known as abortive poliomyelitis, and recovered without ever being diagnosed. With symptoms ranging from a sore throat to diarrhea, this form of the disease could well be mistaken for a summer cold or stomach virus.

A small percentage of parents, like Norma's mother, believed in the efficacy of the vaccine available at the time and sought the injectible live virus as protection. The more successful vaccine, a killed virus developed by Jonas Salk, wasn't deemed safe for wide distribution until 1955. Most simply curtailed their children's contact with people who had been around the polio victim for at least two weeks, which was the incubation period for the disease. The family of the polio victim went through a self-imposed quarantine during the incubation period, particularly if they had other children at home. In some cases, I'm sure the mental scars from the isolation these families endured were comparable to those of the polio victims themselves.

As a county health officer I reported any cases of polio for public record, which usually set off a chain of events that tainted the carefree days of summer for children who'd been in contact with those diagnosed. For a couple of weeks after the cases were diagnosed, the City shut down the swimming pool, thought to be a link to the spread of the disease.

An outbreak of paralytic poliomyelitis put fear into a community like no other infectious disease because it appeared to target children, with rare cases occurring among teenagers. The sudden onset of the disease, beginning with symptoms of the common cold, such as sore throat and headache, could be fatefully deceptive. When a stiff neck and impaired response to simple reflex tests accompanied these symptoms, I urged parents to transport a child to the nearest hospital equipped for more thorough diagnosis and treatment of polio. Some chose the Dallas area, some Houston, others went to Louisiana.

In the case of a five-year-old named Kenneth Dorsett, they chose Hedgecroft, a seventy-bed hospital in Houston dedicated to acute care of polio and other respiratory and spinal diseases. Fortunately for Ken, his paralysis was a result of spinal poliomyelitis; had it been bulbar poliomyelitis, which attacked respiratory and vasomotor centers of the body—most tragically the patient's ability to breathe—the outlook for Ken would have been undeniably grim. Life sustained by an iron lung, a gargantuan predecessor to the light hoses and plastic now housing portable respirators, was the only alternative for victims of bulbar poliomyelitis. Though he escaped the horribly-restricted life such dependence incurred, Ken's extensive stay in the children's ward at Hedgecroft left an indelible imprint.

The 'persevering and systematic movements' prescribed for paralysis victims at the turn of the century may have evolved into what is now considered physical therapy, yet it hardly describes Ken Dorsett's experience at Hedgecroft. "They would put you on a hard, foam-rubber bed—strap you down at the knees and waist, then the bed would tilt up to stand you upright and they could bend and flex your limbs, to try to straighten them. To hear these kids screaming when they would strap them down."

Even forty-five years later, Ken's voice broke as he recalled the tortured cries of those children.

Amazingly, Ken's memories of the months he spent at the Houston hospital were punctuated with some of the happier moments in his life, such as daily visits from his mother, who rented a room down the street from the hospital to be closer to him, and a very special get-well card from the Nacogdoches Fire Department. The early part of 1953 marked a historic moment for the Fire Department, having just purchased its first truck with an electric ladder. When Ken received a picture of the truck, signed by the fire chief, it was the beginning of a poignant relationship between the future poster child for the March of Dimes and the Fire Department.

In my experience, the debilitating effect of polio on the victim physically often contrasted sharply with immense psychological, or if you will, moral, courage. This may have been a by-product of the times, the need of the sons and daughters of the community to lead productive lives in spite of handicaps. Local newspaper accounts chronicled Ken's accomplishments throughout his life, from being a leader in FFA as a teen to his acumen in the business world as owner of a successful watch repair business.

Ken recalled his childhood as being no different than that of most country boys, with slight modifications in the way he performed chores.

"My main job on our dairy farm was feeding the baby calves. I couldn't carry all the buckets at one time, so I'd put the buckets in a little red wagon, tie one end of a rope to the wagon and the other to my waist and take off to feed the calves." The heavy steel of braces on Ken's legs presented no less of a problem when driving his father's tractor—he simply lifted a leg with both hands if he needed to press the brake or the clutch.

With no major outbreaks of polio in America since the fifties, a false sense of security exists among today's parents of young children. Though current infant immunization schedules include administering a version of Salk's oral vaccine, a growing number of practitioners as well as lay people question the need for this; after all, in the words of Lange's *Current Medical Diagnosis and Treatment,* "Wild poliovirus disease has been eradicated from the Western hemisphere."

I would say to them, we should not let our guard down against a disease that has robbed so many of the ability to walk or breathe on their own. The Center for Disease Control keeps samples of the influenza virus that devastated the world in 1918 under lock and key; we should treat the disease called poliomyelitis with no less respect.

# CHAPTER VII

## The Pet

The main lending institution in a small East Texas town during the forties and fifties, Chireno State Bank gave the appearance of solidity and conformity. So did its president, H.V. Hall. One of the first calls I received from H.V. however, revealed to me a personality that no building—not even the tallest skyscraper in Houston—could contain or reflect, because he was simply larger than life.

The red brick one-story building that employed one teller and one clerk when I first started going to Chireno observed typical bankers' hours, nine to three. A room at the back served as a small restaurant where H.V. held court. When he wasn't advising farmers about how far they should invest savings toward crops yet to be sown, his deep laugh and cigar smoke reminded everyone in the lobby of his presence. As shrewd as any bank president when it came to the stockholders' investments, he nonetheless pulled cash out of his own pocket when people down on their luck approached him. He took their word as a promissory note. His accomplishments in finance management earned him a place of respect in and beyond the community, but it was his generous nature that endeared him to most, including me.

This is not to say that H.V. was sweetness and light; my first meeting with him would argue the opposite. He wanted me to remove a cast that covered his leg from mid-thigh to his ankle, which had been set to keep him from flexing a fractured patella.

H.V.'s accent was pronounced, even for East Texas. "I need you to take this cast off mah leg," he said.

I asked him who'd put it on.

"Doc Pennington."

"Well, he'll have to take it off."

"I can't find him and I'm goin' to a banker's meetin' in Dallas. I want it off."

I tried to convince him it was to his benefit to have it removed by the physician that placed it.

Like many fair-complected people, when his temper flared, his face became a barometer. The greater the velocity of crimson that rose from his collar to his receding hairline, the greater the warning for the recipient of his wrath. "If ya don't take it off, I'm gonna whup ya."

I decided to call his bluff. "You'll just have to get after it. If I don't take it off, you're gonna "whup" me and if I do, Pennington will "whup" me. That's the way it is."

Anyone overhearing our encounter would have thought we were neighbors squabbling over a stray cow; our bare-knuckles conversation belied any semblance of the professional roles we represented in the community.

Unexpectedly, he chuckled.

"I'm not accustomed to this kind of treatment. I was raised a pet." In a conciliatory tone that told me he respected my calling his bluff, he explained that he was used to getting what he wanted most of his life. I had little doubt after our first meeting that very few people denied him or stood up to him in disagreement. I also suspected that he rarely backed down as humbly as he did with me that day. The only way I knew to acknowledge his opening up to me without appearing to patronize him was to tell him a little about myself. Within a few minutes, we were bragging and joking as though we'd grown up together, kicking rocks along the main street of Chireno. Before I admitted to having a few more housecalls to make, I extended an offer of my services for future needs. "I know Doc Pennington and he's a fine doctor," I added. We shook hands and he sought Pennington to remove the cast.

I was so taken with "I was raised a pet" that I used it on occasion when I didn't get what I wanted. I believe H.V. had far more luck with it than I did.

H.V. often called me to see a patient who couldn't afford to call a doctor. This might include a dear friend, an acquaintance or someone who worked for him. He'd wait for me to drive up, ride with me to give directions, and pay my bill when I drove him back to the bank. Just when I thought I knew what to expect from him, he'd pull the proverbial rabbit out of his hat. And if I expected the rabbit to be white, it would be most likely be spotted.

One sunny June day we were enroute to see a patient when he had me stop next to a planted corn field where a tenant farmer was plowing. H.V. had barely emerged from the car when the farmer stopped his plowing and met him over the fence.

"You gettin' the corners clean?" I heard H.V. ask the man.

"Yes sir, Mr. Hall."

"You know I'm keeping an eye on you," H.V. continued.

The man replied, "Yes sir, I know that very thing," before they parted.

When he got back in the car I asked H.V. what he meant when he said he was watching the man.

"You know about that TV aerial on my house?" he asked me.

Of course I had noticed it. H.V. was probably the only one with a television within a thirty-five-mile radius. "I got these guys workin' the fields believin' I can keep track of what they're doin' through that aerial. They think I can watch them on my TV."

One evening just before dark H.V. called me to come out and see an old friend of his because Bo was getting sicker by the day. H.V. had genuine affection for the elderly black man living alone in a simple cabin in the woods. The way to the cabin was lined with old oaks, majestic in their domination of that part of the woods. The virgin pine timber that had once surrounded the home place had been cleared during the war by German POWs, allowing the hardwood timber to flourish and crown so that the whole area reminded me of something out of the forgotten south, like a scene from *Gone with the Wind*.

As I followed H.V. up the steps to the only door, a stillness about the place emphasized its air of solemnity. The only sound inside was Bo's ragged breathing.

Inside, a frail, white-whiskered man lay propped on an uneven mattress. From a supine position he extended a bony hand in greeting. Talking taxed him yet he accepted my probing and questions with patience borne of a lifetime of waiting on others.

After listening to his heart and lungs, I performed some simple tests. It soon became apparent to me that H.V.'s old friend wasn't just sick—he was entering the terminal stages of a cancer that had been diagnosed months earlier. I told him I had something in my bag to ease the pain and would be back after I prepared an injection. In those days, I carried granular morphine in my bag. It would be easier for me to prepare the injection in the dusky daylight outside than by the unsteady light from his lamp, I explained to him. I had another reason for stepping outside and motioned H.V. to follow.

As soon as we walked a few paces from the cabin, I broke the news to him that Bo was dying.

H.V.'s upper lip turned white with anger. "Well that's a hell of a note."

Spiked by extreme frustration at his own helplessness in alleviating his friend's suffering, his next words raked over me like a wood rasp. "Can't you give him a shot, something strong enough to put him out of his misery?"

I strained to keep my voice low. "I can't do that; it's illegal and besides that, it's wrong."

"What's the matter with you—ain't you got no hawt?"

"Yeah, I got a heart." I understood H.V.'s reasoning but stammered trying to get him to see mine. "It g-goes against the ethics of mankind," I argued.

"Well, it ain't against mine. Hand it over and I'll give him the shot."

"I can't do that either, H.V."

"So what do you intend to do?"

I told him I'd ease Bo with a dose of morphine for now and leave him with a prescription.

"Hell, if that's all you're gonna do, go ahead." He turned away, grinding a heel in disgust.

After injecting a half grain of morphine into the man and

leaving him with a prescription for Demerol, we started back to the car. It was a long walk, made more difficult by failing light, not to mention our crushed spirits. Rather than hunt a gap in the barbed-wire fence between the cabin and the road, we looked for the uneven steps of the crudely-built stile we'd used earlier to cross the fence. My hands full, H.V. held a lantern to light the way.

Just in front of the stile, he stopped. His voice was low, huskier than usual, which didn't help my nerves. The combination of shadows dancing on his face and the gravity of his voice raised the hair on the back of my neck.

"Now I want you to tell me," he spoke plainly. "Don't fool me. How long before he gonna die?"

It took me a few seconds to realize that he thought the shot I gave the patient was a lethal injection.

"My gosh, H.V., I didn't give him something to kill him," I protested.

"The hell you didn't."

As I drove back to town in my car, I don't know what was darker, the road or my thoughts. The low whine of the engine gathering speed helped to form a prayer that didn't leave my thoughts that night: 'God, please don't let that patient die before morning.'

If the patient didn't make it through the night, I had no doubt H.V. would think he talked me into a lethal dose after all, and he would spread the word. "If a patient needs to be put out of his misery, call Dr. Taylor."

Fortunately, Bo lived through the night, countermanding H.V.'s initial perception of how far I would stretch the physician's oath.

As excitable and outspoken as H.V. was, when an occasion arose involving his family, he could be as subtle as peach fuzz.

He was particularly fond of an aunt who was in her nineties at the time I was called to see her. She lived in the family home, one of the more stately residences in Chireno, if not the largest.

Before he took me to the big house on the hill, he told me she'd asked him how much I charge for housecalls.

"What'd you tell her? " I asked H.V., hoping he didn't quote my standard fee for people I didn't know. He'd heard me say "a dollar a mile, 50 cents a gate" a few times.

"Thee dollars," he said in that brogue that pronounced "three" without the "r." "She thinks that's about all you're worth, so if she asks you what you charge, that's what you tell her 'cause she shore won't pay you a dollar a mile."

She had the usual complaints of extreme age, arthritis and lack of energy. Mostly, she suffered from too much time to dwell on her discomfort and not enough stimulation from visitors. My exam was cursory, owing to the production she made of putting on coffee to serve and putting out feelers for the news about Nacogdoches. When I got up to leave and she asked how much she owed me, I replied as coached. "Three dollars." As H.V. had warned me, she muttered something like "That's about all a doctor's worth," as she dug into a jar for the money. I didn't take it personally but I could see where H.V. had learned to be outspoken. Before I headed back for Nacogdoches that day, he tried to give me some cash, which I refused. The afternoon had been entertaining, I told him, and I meant it.

One Saturday, close to noon, we stopped in to see the aunt. As we sat around the kitchen table, I asked her to what she attributed her long life.

"Drinking milk from one certain cow and water from one certain well," she answered without hesitation. I've asked many patients this same question with no two replies being the same. Hers was one of the most original.

As we started to leave, our talk turned to football. H.V. and I debated the outcome of an eagerly-anticipated game between SMU and Texas.

She interrupted us. "I want to tell you boys somethin'." Though I was approaching forty, under her glare I felt like a boy. "The other day I was listenin' to the finest prayer on the radio. I'd just gotten into the mood of it when they quit prayin' and commenced to hollerin' for some ball game." In her estimation, games didn't rate serious contemplation, much less prayer. "Prayin' before a ball game," she said with such disgust I thought she was going to spit. "I know durn well that the Lord's goin' to strike 'em dead one day—that's the worst thing I ever heard of."

Her sentiments regarding prayer at sports functions stemmed from a generation that viewed it as blasphemous to pray in the same breath as you would cheer a team to victory. How ironic that her distaste for the practice is echoed today among those who want to ban it from high school football games for opposite reasons.

# CHAPTER VIII

# Cardinal Rule #1

From my days of undergraduate classroom lecture and nights of sharing intern quarters over a psychiatric ward at Parkland Hospital to the culmination of a thirty-nine-year medical practice, I developed an appreciation for certain habits I recommend to men and women in general. These habits, or recommended behaviors, are firmly ensconced in my mind as cardinal rules of life.

A rule of life I think imperative for human beings of civilized and uncivilized nations alike, if good health is desired, tops my list: Wash your hands frequently.

In medical school, and later as interns, we scrubbed before going to the lab, after working in the lab, prior to eating, after eating, etc.; it was drilled into us to regard our hands as instruments that should be kept immaculate. This was the best defense against the spread of microorganisms ranging from anaerobic bacteria such as streptococci to the pathogen *Trichophyton rubrum,* the fungal agent most often associated with ringworm.

Think about it. On an average day, the number of hands that will touch currency exchanged at a supermarket, or that your toddler will encounter in play at the daycare center that houses twenty other toddlers—the spread of germs in such a way is like raindrops on the ocean, their impact on the ocean seemingly insignificant but their assimilation inevitable.

A parting comment my close friends and family have come to expect from me is a subtle reminder of this rule. "Be good," I counsel and after a pause, I add, "If you can't be good, be sanitary."

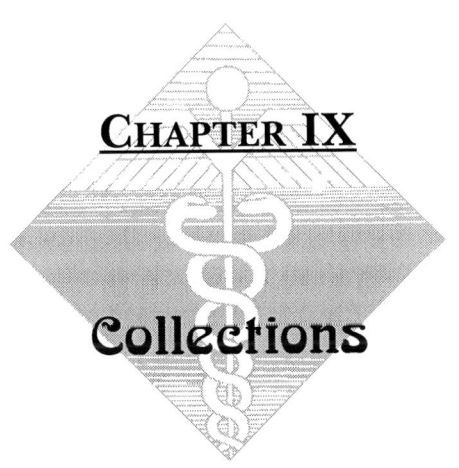

# Chapter IX

# Collections

As one of the hands at my father's flour mill in Denton during the Depression, part of my job was weighing the raw wheat when farmers brought it in by the truck load and determining how much we would pay them. These men in their faded overalls knew I was the mill owner's son and they took my word as a non-negotiable price. Many of these men stood around without shoes. It was clear to me, even as innocent as I was to the ways of the world, that these people didn't have nearly as good a life as I did. For this reason, and the fact that they treated me as an equal, I always gave them more than what my father had designated we could pay per bushel. He never knew that I overpaid them; they didn't either; a lot of them couldn't read and had to trust my reading the scales correctly. My father was a successful businessman in part because once he set a price, he didn't budge when it came to collecting. I don't regret that I did not inherit this trait from him; though I'll never be the financial success he was, I have all that matters, as well as some mental portraits of patients that have enriched my life beyond measure.

When it came to running my practice, my books would probably have been in the red if not for my office manager and right hand, a tall, lanky young nurse named Lucy Koonce Lazarine. Without hesitation, I can say that no other nurse of my acquaintance can touch Lucy professionally. Her skill in sizing up the needs of patients, whether they were walk-ins or had appointments, and shuttling them through the process—from exam to paperwork to payment—was the oil that made the wheel of office visits turn with the greatest efficiency.

This gift of efficiency extends to Lucy's personality as well. She believes in calling it like she sees it, with no apologies or "buttering up" the facts. Just the other day, she asked me, "You know why you never made any money in your practice?"

I stepped willingly into the trap. "No, Lucy. Why didn't I make any money?"

"You remember the man that was Pennington's patient? Came to see you because he couldn't pay Pennington's bill."

Something was vaguely familiar about the scenario. I told her to go on.

"You asked him if he really wanted you to look at him or if he wanted Pennington. He said he'd like to go to him but Pennington wanted money. So you fished a ten out of your pocket, handed it to him, and told him to go see Dr. Pennington."

Payment for services rendered was never a concern to me. If a patient couldn't pay and it was obvious that it was because he couldn't afford to, I didn't expect payment. Most of the patients I saw on housecalls offered to pay me immediately, but there were a few exceptions, not only in the form of payment but the way in which it was rendered.

One of the more unexpected attempts to settle a bill came from a woman of means if not manners.

As I was leaving the hospital one evening, she hailed me from her car, parked just a few feet away. I was ready to go home, anxious to unwind after a long day. When I saw who it was I almost turned and went back to the hospital, ready to swear I heard someone call me from the emergency entrance.

Though I had treated her entire family for various ailments over a span of some months, neither she nor her husband had paid my fee on any of those occasions. Knowing the family to be wealthy by the day's standards, I allowed this to continue without comment when they sought my services, sure that I would be compensated by payment in the mailbox eventually.

If she had been alone, I probably would have gone back to the hospital until she left. But she had a child with her and asked me to examine him right then. The ailment was minor, but not so my temper after realizing that she had probably staked out my car and knew that I wouldn't refuse to see the child.

Up until then, I had never asked a patient for payment. While part of me disliked being taken advantage of, another part of me despised asking for money. After diagnosing the child's problem, I said in a half-bantering tone, "You caught me here in the parking lot. You always manage to catch me at an inconvenient time—by the way, you haven't paid me for any visits and I know your family is well off."

Almost immediately she said, "Stand inside my car door and hide me for a minute. I'll give you some money."

My curiosity roused, I waited beside the open door. Maybe she kept a stash of cash under the seat and didn't want anyone to see where she pulled it from. Before I had time to conjure another explanation in my mind, up went her skirt, down came her panties, and without so much as a "pardon me" she reached into her vagina and pulled out a hundred dollar bill.

Perhaps my status as her physician made this seem a perfectly natural action to her. I don't remember what was said after that. Maybe I managed a "thanks" as I took the bill from her, holding it gingerly by one corner.

Like a new father carrying a sodden diaper, I carried it back to the hospital emergency room. I had the attention of all on duty that night. They watched as I went to a sink, washed the bill with soap and warm water, patted it dry with a towel, and took it to the cashier to ask for change.

It was the first and last time I reminded a patient who owed me money.

Characteristic of East Texans during the early years of my practice, offers of payment came with some rather original substitutions for money.

After one case in which I performed a hernia repair, the patient, though extremely grateful, reported with sincere regret that he had no money. This was fine by me but it seemed to lay heavy on his conscience until an idea occurred to him.

"If you ever need a witness, let me know."

Though I've never needed anyone to 'be' a witness for me, so earnest was this man that I've turned this concept over in my mind many times during the years since then. Sometimes it helps to pass some of the longer moments of forced captivity, like during the Sunday sermon that goes past noon while my gastrointestinal tract reminds me that I haven't eaten since the night before.

First prize for the most creative form of escaping payment I would have to award to Dick Davis, a well-known citizen of Chireno.

After performing successful surgery on his wife, I paid a visit to them to see how she was doing. Eventually, the subject of the bill came up. Dick had been mulling over this and devised a unique installment plan.

"I'll pay ya a little bit now, and I'll pay ya a little bit every time I see ya. But if I ain't got no money when we meet up, I'll put my hands over my eyes like this so that ya won't catch me goin' against my word."

Of course, I interpreted this to mean that Dick was going to pay me a little every time our paths crossed, whether it was in the drugstore, on the street, or in my office. To avoid paying me, he simply shielded his eyes in my presence so he could honestly say he didn't see me. A man of his word, he didn't look at me until he could pay me.

# CHAPTER X

# Cardinal Rule #2

I can still hear the booming voice of my bacteriology professor waking me from a lecture-induced stupor one long afternoon during freshman classes at Baylor. We were all about to nod off over our notes when Dr. Carter shouted "Don't EVER do this!"

"A seemingly harmless act," he continues, "but plucking hair from the inside of your nose can open an avenue for a virulent form of streptococci to get in the bloodstream, via the vessels that drain into the cavernous sinuses just above the mouth." Untreated, he warns, such invasion of these cavities can result in death. For the same reason, an abscess in the nasal cavity should be treated with great caution.

I'm not advocating the Howard Hughes approach to avoiding the microscopic dangers that abound in the world today. Life as a phobic recluse is hardly a life. However, we would be worse than foolish to ignore the six-o'clock news that reports deaths resulting from a flesh-eating bacteria contracted from swimming in stagnant water.

It was the fall of 1940. My medical internship with Parkland included working the night shift in Parkland's emergency room for several months. One such shift began on a deceptively calm note, conducive to a lonely intern daydreaming about what he would do when his shift ended. A call from the Dallas Fire Department ended any further speculation about life after my

shift. Parkland—at that time the city's only charity hospital—
had been contacted to receive the victims of a fire that had broken out at a Red Cross shelter for indigent men. Volunteers at
the site figured the fire that swept through the warehouse-size
building was started by a cigarette smoldering in the bedding,
which consisted of loose hay. Given the lower humidity of the
autumn night air and the draftiness of the warehouse, once it
broke into flame, the fire spread quickly among the sleeping
occupants. The only intern on ER duty, I went to the hospital
operator and had her notify all available medical staff in the
hospital of the incoming emergency. As a team of doctors, nurses, orderlies and myself assembled in the ER, I felt more than an
adrenaline rush anticipating the part we were about to play in
the unfolding drama. Youth and inexperience made me blissful-
ly confident that we were ready for whatever came through the
double doors at the other end of the emergency room. How
soon I was to be educated to the contrary.

When the first ambulance appeared, a man emerged with
the skin dangling from his palms, caused by trying to snuff the
fire out with nothing but his hands. "Better get ready for a
bunch more," the ambulance driver warned before he closed the
doors and raced back to the shelter. Every available ambulance
responded, including several owned and operated by funeral
homes. They deposited close to thirty victims in the ER that
night, ranging from a few who wobbled in, disoriented from
smoke inhalation but relatively unscathed by flames, to the
stretcher-borne majority who relied on all of us—medical staff,
orderlies, and fellow indigents—to make things right for them.
Those who were conscious reminded us that pain in itself is life-
threatening, their wails subdued by failing strength while we
worked feverishly to attend the unconscious first. We'd stock-
piled plasma for use during such an emergency and it undoubt-
edly saved a few lives by bringing the patients out of shock, but
we lost probably ten percent of those brought to us.

It remains one of the more enlightening experiences of my
professional life; not only was it my first time to witness such a
grisly parade of charred, writhing figures, the accompanying
smells and sounds enough to bring on nausea among the most
hardened medical staff, but it was also the first time I realized

the far-reaching consequences of the Depression. Many of the victims I attended in various stages of treatment, whether to give transfusions or apply dressings, I talked to as I worked. I offered to write letters for those who apparently would not last the night. As they gave me their names and told me something about themselves, I was amazed by the spectrum of talented, well-educated individuals. From bankers to bakers, these men had once been productive, some of them even immensely successful members of society. The domino effect of our failed economy wiped out more than ambitions. Many had lost spouses and children, through enforced separation and alienation. I blinked often to stifle my own tears, overwhelmed by the discovery that men who could have been one of my family or friends had been reduced to this level of misery.

Any doctor who has worked shifts in an emergency room or with a trauma unit can attest to the strength of human will and endurance in surviving and overcoming injury, both internal and external. This introduction to human suffering of such magnitude instilled in me a belief that beneath the epidermal layers we call skin and deeper than the vascular and muscular networks that surround our vital organs, our bodies harbor a survival mechanism that some call the human spirit. This spirit allows us to endure unimaginable pain, whether the source is the bone-crunching clinch of machinery in an industrial accident or the flesh-liquefying sear of flames from a warehouse fire.

But the injury we have most to fear when it comes to breaking down our fragile human shell is invisible to the naked eye, is often self-sustained, and could be prevented by informed behavior.

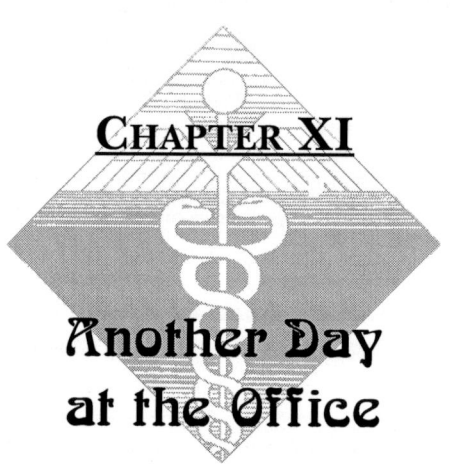

# CHAPTER XI

# Another Day
# at the Office

I've never known a doctor who wasn't a football fan. College football in particular can become an obsession among us. For one colleague who ran a nerve clinic, the lure of a game between SMU and Texas A&M was too much to resist.

Most doctors' offices closed on Saturday afternoons. This young psychiatrist showed up for work as usual, crisply attired in a new white lab coat, expecting one or two patients in the waiting room. Anticipating that he would close early to get on the road for the game, he opened the door to the waiting room to find fifteen patients staring at him.

As he retreated to the back of the office, he told his nurse, "You've got to get some of these patients to leave."

"I can't do that," she said, oblivious to his distress. "Some of them have been waiting an hour to see you."

Explaining why he couldn't spend time with all of the patients, the doctor paused, expecting the nurse to come up with a solution for him. She expressed regret but couldn't see how he was going to turn away any of them.

Desperation set in. Without telling the nurse his intention, he strolled back out to the waiting room, smiling at the patients. Within a few seconds, his arms jerked spasmodically and he slid to the floor in a faked convulsion that would have fooled the senior staff at Johns Hopkins. The only thing he left out was biting

*Lucy Koonce Lazarine at Bailey St. entrance to clinic, c. early fifties.*

his tongue, though he managed to slobber a little, soiling the white lab coat.

After a minute or two he got up, brushed himself off, and looked around the waiting room as if nothing had happened. Nearly all of the patients got up to leave, a few brave ones stopping long enough to make an appointment for the following week. The nurse cleared the room by saying, "I'm sorry but when the doctor's tired and overworked he has these seizures."

Before Dr. Walter B. Allen and I built a clinic across from Memorial Hospital in 1952, I didn't see patients in an office setting consistently enough to worry about emptying a waiting room. The space I shared with Sarah above Swift Brothers and Smith Pharmacy was typical of most doctors' offices: A small suite of rooms with no air conditioning, it had a few straight-back chairs in the front room for whites and a bench outside designated as the "colored" waiting room. Though I was accustomed to seeing segregation to some extent all my life, it was

*Dr. Walter B. Allen at his desk in the clinic he shared
with the author on Bailey Street, c. 1950s.*

strange to me that everyone, blacks included, seemed to accept
this order of service without question.

It seems so unbelievable now, but when I approved the
architect's drawing for the clinic on Bailey in 1952, it included a
separate entrance and waiting room for blacks. Until the sixties,
my office was typical of most establishments in town regarding
segregation. The fact that most of the black families seemed
comfortable with this segregation did not make it any less abhor-
rent in hindsight. When we first tried to integrate the waiting
rooms, one of my most loyal employees threatened to walk out
because she "wasn't raised for the races to mix in such a way."
After a lot of discussion among our small staff, she finally agreed
to stay and follow our lead in the transition.

We were open from 8:00 A.M. until no more came in the
door, sometimes until 9:00 P.M., Monday through Friday, usually
closing at noon on Saturday. Sarah had a special room for exam-
ining her pediatric patients, and observed different office hours

than I did. Between Sally and the arrival of our son, Tom, in 1951, she found the role of mother every bit as demanding as that of physician. For the first few years, Dr. Allen shared the building with us, bringing his wife in as a lab technician and with the fees for x-rays and lab work designated to go back into the building, we paid for the building within five years. Not only did we share office staff and supplies, but I occasionally gave him credit when treating children. If an injection was indicated, I'd sometimes tell the child, "If it hurts, remember: Dr. Allen gave you the shot."

Before Medicare, insurance and the web of paperwork now associated with processing patients for payment, the office ran efficiently with a staff of two receptionists, two bookkeepers, and two nurses. Patients usually came in without appointments and we always managed to see them within a reasonable time. The college campus had a clinic, but occasionally students came to us and we treated them at no charge. Drop-ins were inevitable, particularly people from out of town because of our proximity to the university and the hospital, I suppose.

A drop-in proved to be one of the few fatalities I had at the office. A couple from Pennsylvania were passing through on their way to visit the college when chest pains struck the man, who was driving. Spotting my sign, he barely managed to park and get into the office before a massive coronary overtook him in the exam room. Within minutes he died, unresponsive to our CPR attempts.

One of my most dedicated nurses said you have to love people to see some of the patients we did in the early days on Bailey and not become discouraged about the human race. A case in point involved a young boy we treated for numerous deficiencies, brought on by what appeared to be malnutrition. This was not a common occurrence among the patients I visited in East Texas, where people who were poor may do without shoes but always had the means to put nutritious food on the table. His family lived in a community east of town that believed a cult had put an irreversible curse on them. Whether it was the influence of superstition spurred by a clannish community or simple ignorance and neglect, we'll never know what happened after the boy left our office. A family member leaked details of a prophecy that their first male child would not live to see his teen years to my nurse. Not long after their visit to our office, we heard that the boy died, supposedly after a lingering illness of undetermined origin. Though the family mourned his passing, they seemed to accept that this was their due. Such a destructive mindset, especially when the young and frail are in its path, haunts me to this day.

As the news spread among my patients that not only was I a family doctor, but that I could alleviate the pain of childbirth and remained with the mother after childbirth to insure proper post-partem care, my practice grew exponentially in the area of gynecology and obstetrics. Nothing pleased me more professionally-speaking than to see a woman through an uncomplicated pregnancy and delivery. Many women who did not seek total nine-month care throughout a first pregnancy came to me for regular check-ups for successive pregnancies, an indication of the changing attitude toward prenatal care.

I never delivered a baby at the office. If a woman was in labor when she came to the office, we always managed to get her across the street to the hospital in plenty of time for the traditional setting of a delivery. If there were no complications she usually had a three to four-day stay in the hospital, released only after nurses had her walking and regaining strength. In the case of Cesarean sections, the hospital stay averaged seven to ten days.

A number of our patients confessed reliance on home remedies, usually after the remedy failed to work or made the condition they hoped to cure worse. Whiskey, whether it was the "John Paul Jones" variety sold in the drugstore, or of the homemade vintage, accounted for the main ingredient of home remedies for everything from a cough to angina pain. One of our favorite "confessions" came from a lady who was disturbed by her behavior after taking a home remedy for a cough.

What was in the formula? I asked.

Honey, lemon juice, peppermint candy, and a little whiskey, she replied.

Did it help the cough? I prompted.

It did more than that, she said, her face flushed with embarrassment. I took another dose after the first one 'cause I didn't want the cough to come back. The next thing I knew, I was sit-tin' on the back steps with a bunch of headless chickens runnin' around the yard 'cause I'd wrung their necks.

The lady, a teetotaler, had gotten drunk on the home remedy.

A habit I developed during my practice has come back to haunt me in recent years, especially when I attend social events where I run into many of my former patients. Not so long ago, I was honored to speak at an anniversary celebration of the hospital's founding. Since the hospital advertised that there would be special recognition of all those born in the facility, there was quite a gathering of mothers and offspring, a great many of whom I delivered. Women I had not seen since their babies' deliveries, some more than thirty-five years ago, sought me with the enthusiastic greeting, "Remember me? You used to call me 'Sunshine'!" Of course, I had to smile and nod. How could I forget Sunshine; nearly every woman I helped through a pregnancy I had addressed as such, particularly when their names didn't come to me easily.

Writing prescriptions in the early days of my practice differed dramatically from what is done now. Medical schools in the forties drilled students in pharmacology by requiring them write the formulas on prescription pads, with exact quantities and order of components listed for a pharmacist to fill. Due to the variety of problems and spectrum of patients I treated over the years, I refined these formulas and developed some of my own, based on individual response to the remedy.

I developed a particularly effective remedy for "honeymoon bladder," a condition brought on by irritation of the vagina through frequent sexual activity, which produces the urgency to urinate more than normal. I wrote the prescription as such: Four drams each of tincture of hyocyamus and potassium citrate, sufficient quantity four ounces of elixir phenobarbitol; directions: 1 teaspoon in water every 3 hours as needed for urgency to void.

The arrival of Nick the Greek brought East Texas physicians into the twentieth century when it came to writing prescriptions.

*Dr. Sarah Ferguson, pediatrician in residence at the Bailey clinic, c. mid-fifties.*

Nick Kinakis was the first "detail man"—a slang term in the medical community for pharmaceutical representatives—to visit my office in Nacogdoches. Before I opened the clinic, his route and reputation as one of the most knowledgeable drug salesmen in East Texas were well-established. As the rapidly-growing industry of ready-made drugs of varying dosage and mediums was brought directly to our offices via such salesmen, physicians gladly phased out time-consuming, detailed formulas for the convenience and accuracy of referring to one of these brand-name drugs on the prescription. Representing one of the largest and most well-known pharmaceutical companies in operation today, Nick's training in the field had been intense, but he did more than just present a product; he'd memorized inert and active ingredients' roles and proportions as well as common side effects to watch for and could follow the most complicated query of any physician I knew. More amazing than his knowledge of pharmaceuticals however, were Nick's connections: Anything you wanted, Nick could procure.

A man of impeccable taste in suits, cars, jewelry, and later, antiques, he always arrived at the office in great style. He would carry most of his samples and literature in a large black leather valise. After he displayed the latest the company had to offer, he would dig deep into the bag and say something like, "How about something to bring a spark to your wife's eyes?" and produce a flawless 1/2-carat diamond. "Put that under her pillow tonight and you'll both be happy," he'd continue. If you simply mentioned you liked a certain model car, Nick would offer to find it and make a deal for you.

Though retired now, Nick remains an active figure in the community. During his career as a detail man, he earned numerous awards for excellence in his service to the company. He also made a lot of friends among physicians, perhaps epitomized by the gift of a personal portrait made to him by Dr. Denton Cooley in Houston during the late seventies. World traveler and salesman extraordinaire, he is simply Nick the Greek to those of us who have known him these forty-plus years.

# CHAPTER XII

# Surround Yourself
# with the Best

Before we were doctors, we were interns.

To define an internship as I experienced it at Parkland has to include a comradeship with other young men in which we shared lodging, notes, and antics, much as we had in our years in medical school. The main difference between being a medical student and an intern involved more caution when we pulled pranks, a sign of gradual acceptance of the mantle of maturity we acquired from the stern, older men we studied under.

We knew enough not to take our place in Parkland for granted; after all, the student had to overcome a significant intellectual hurdle to reach such status, which could be wiped out with one misstep around the physicians who taught us. But as inevitably as young men in cloistered environments often digress to childish or daring pranks, so we as interns followed suit.

The summer of 1940 in Dallas offered no surprises where heat was concerned. Air conditioning was non-existent in the interns' quarters, located on the floor above the psychiatric ward of Parkland. This alone made sleeping difficult some nights, due to the noise as much as the heat drifting through open windows. One particular night we were "serenaded" by the ranting of a psychiatric patient, who called incessantly for St. Peter.

The eerie whine of the patient's voice seemed buoyed by the hot night air, loud enough to galvanize us into action. Someone located a small bell and some string. While the rest of us gathered at the window overlooking the patient's room, our mastermind-intern lowered the bell until it was adjacent to the patient's window and jiggled it. In a soft, high-pitched voice, he called down to the patient, "Do you hear the bell?", repeating this several times until the patient answered hesitantly, "Yes, I hear the bell."

The intern's voice deepened dramatically. "This is St. Peter and if you don't keep it quiet down there, you're not getting in up here!"

We heard no more from the patient that night and as we followed the physician on rounds the next morning, we weren't sure which patient it was until the doctor picked up a chart and read aloud, "Patient called out several times during night. Claims to have had conversation with St. Peter."

Like most young interns, I believed that I knew everything when I graduated from medical school. What I lacked in experience, Parkland was fortunate to gain in talent and enthusiasm, in my mind. How quickly such preconceived notions are dashed.

It was a slow night in the emergency room. Having worked ER for several months, I had settled into a routine that was partly to blame for my actions that night. Routine often triggered boredom for me in those days. I joked with the ambulance driver to pass the time until we got a call from the hospital switchboard with the news of a shooting on Lemon Avenue, to send the ambulance right away. I had accompanied the driver on several calls, not because it was required but for the thrill of the ride. What could be more exciting than flying through intersections in downtown Dallas, lights flashing and siren blaring, with no restrictions whatsoever? The only thing better would be driving the ambulance, I decided.

A few steps ahead of the driver, I bolted for the exit, grabbing his uniform cap from a peg by the door on the way out. I ignored his protests until I was in the driver's seat, starting the engine and throwing it into gear, during which time all he could do was climb into the passenger side and hold on. After he said something like "Are you crazy?" for the third time I retorted, "I just want you to see what it's like to ride in an ambulance with a driver like you."

Before the age of EMTs and the sophisticated portable

equipment found in them today, ambulances were more like large station wagons simply outfitted for transporting a patient as quickly as possible to the hospital. The driver had little if any medical training; his most valuable assets were driving skill, i.e. reflexes, and physical strength to help with loading and unloading patients. Usually, one or two attendants—again, not necessarily with any medical training—accompanied the driver, depending on availability of personnel and the magnitude of the crisis requiring the ambulance.

Consequently, the patient's survival often depended on the speed at which he reached the hospital, where the team of medical personnel and vital equipment waited. Until I drove the ambulance to the site of the shooting that night, I had no concept of the responsibility and perilous duty that defined that driver's job. The sense of exhilaration in speeding through traffic signals died as soon as I had a near-miss with a vehicle that simply pulled out in front of us and froze. Other drivers, not road conditions or maneuvering the ambulance at high speeds, proved to be the number one hazard to the successful transport of a patient. As I heard the displaced driver cry out at one point, "You're gonna get me killed!" I suddenly realized I'd said the same thing when I was a passenger. Knowing we couldn't stop to change places at that point, I promised him he'd be driving on the way back. Only then did I truly respect his skill and the good fortune I had to be working in a place that hired someone of his caliber.

The first time I was asked what advice I would pass on to the physicians of the next century, I feared that nothing from my experiences could relate to the challenges facing the current crop. I was born the year of the first long-distance telephone call, from San Francisco to New York, between Alexander G. Bell and Thomas A. Watson; I began a practice at a time when there was no line of defense against polio, cancer, or heart disease. When I retired, AIDS had debuted and was gaining a reputation as the disease of homosexuals and drug addicts; it would be almost another decade, with the emergence of extraordinary

people like Ryan White and Arthur Ashe—victims of the disease
through transfusions—that such a pedestrian approach to this
disease would be turned around.

In retrospect, the years I practiced medicine saw the advent
of medical discoveries that seem antiquated now, the evolution
of antibiotics perhaps one of the most dramatic examples. How
could anything I've learned be relative to the tasks facing the
laser-wielding surgeons and myriad of specialists who will usher
in a new millennium? After all, the current generation has an
information highway literally in their lap, via portable comput-
ers. The astounding changes wrought in this century—from
horse-drawn carriages to space shuttles—will appear sluggish in
comparison with the technologically-spurred advances that will
develop within the first quarter of the next. I am in awe of a
technique recently described to me by a neurosurgeon who has
perfected an avenue of entry into that least-understood organ,
the brain, with incredible success in the treatment of Bell's Palsy.

I could rely on some adage passed down through generations of Taylors at this point and hope that anyone who reads it
would conclude that it was rather witty, despite the source being
someone who lived through an ignorant time, medically-speak-
ing. Instead, I'll rely on a proverb, of Arabic origin, that has
explained much to me about people in all walks of life:

There are four sorts of men:

He who knows not and knows not he knows not: He is a
    fool—shun him;
He who knows not and knows he knows not: He is
    simple—teach him;
He who knows and knows not he knows: He is asleep—
    wake him;
He who knows and knows he knows: He is wise—follow
    him.

Any success I can claim in the practice of medicine stems
from sizing up other professionals, knowing when to ask for
help, and surrounding myself with people I believe to be the
best at what they do.

"Experience is only too often a repetition of error."—
Truman Blocker, M.D.

These words, meant to impress upon young doctors that they'd better get it right the first time, came from a surgeon who not only excelled in his area of specialty but who shared his technical expertise without reservation. I was one of about a half-dozen wet-behind-the-ears doctors that met the troop trains at San Antonio Aviation Cadet Center (SAACC), to certify, rectify, or deny the medical fitness of the stir-crazy lads who thought they wanted to be Army pilots in 1942. Dr. Truman Blocker, a professor of plastic surgery who'd left a highly-respected position at one of the only two medical schools in Texas to help train physicians at the SAACC's 1,100-bed hospital, was the first doctor to take me under his wing. Guiding me through procedures that weren't written yet in any medical text, this large hulk of a man executed skin grafts with delicate precision; for those of us lucky enough to scrub with him, his words inspired as much awe as his actions.

When a soldier was shipped to our facility with third degree facial burns, I felt great anguish for him upon seeing that he had no eyelids left. To my knowledge, nowhere else on the body could you find skin that matched the eyelid in elasticity so that not only would the graft accentuate the soldier's disfigurement, it would make a simple act like blinking uncomfortable. Col. Blocker informed the surgical crew that assisted him that there was one part of the body that offered the perfect substitute for an eyelid. To our astonishment, he grafted the foreskin of the man's penis to replace the eyelids, the end result a consummate success in restoring function and natural form to the man's face.

Col. Blocker had an unusual way of correlating his medical experience and knowledge into a philosophy of life. While on the subject of rectal surgery one day, he extolled the virtues of the external sphincter anni in words I'll never forget: "[This muscle] is small and insignificant, but upon its integrity lies the basis of our entire social setup." He further explained that if it weren't for the miraculous control that this muscle afforded us, we'd be going around "squirting like geese all the time."

Truman Blocker returned to UT medical school at Galveston after the war to resume teaching for a tragically short time. I regret that I never had the opportunity to work with him again, though he called me a couple of weeks before he died. Despite the fact that he never said it aloud, I surmised that his cancer was terminal, a powerful revelation for me after he told me that he was glad to have known me during my "formative" years as a physician. I never encountered a more decent or thoughtful teacher. A truly gifted man, Blocker was free of the kind of ego that I have seen become a barrier between teacher and pupil or even between colleagues, at a time when sharing their expertise is so critical.

During the fifties and sixties, one of the most popular television westerns introduced an imposing hulk of a man who could roar like the proverbial lion but whose heart always revealed his true character, that of the peaceable lamb. Those who knew him say that the beloved character of Hoss Cartwright, portrayed as a man who gave all that he had for those in need physically or emotionally, was not an act for Dan Blocker. His generous, gentle heart was real. I owe much to his cousin, Truman Blocker, M.D., who also had the distinction of being of a big man, inside and out.

When I had been at SAACC for about a year, another man to whom I am greatly indebted ordered me to undergo a questionable hernia surgery. Just how fortunate this was for me I didn't find out until after I'd transferred from his command.

A general surgeon who had served with distinction in WWI, Col. John McKewen should have been enjoying a southern gentleman's existence in Baton Rouge, Louisiana. Instead, with the outbreak of WWII and his two sons' enlistment, Colonel McKewen left a staff position at LSU and returned to the service to better his chances of keeping in touch with them. He had a closeness to his boys that extended to his treatment of the enlisted men that came through SAACC, where he was Chief of Surgery over the entire hospital. It was this pride in the young men and concern for their welfare that brought me under his scrutiny and inevitably earned me his invaluable support.

As naive as I was about some aspects of life under Uncle Sam, I knew that maintaining an air of respect toward a higher-ranking officer, no matter what I thought of him personally, was crucial to my professional if not physical survival. Whether this came from being the eldest son and enduring a strict upbringing or if it evolved within the highly-competitive atmosphere of medical school, where insubordination toward a professor was as good an excuse as any to weed out students, I can't say. This lesson served me well one particular day in 1943.

During rounds in the hospital, I walked up on a major berating a private for not snapping to attention. I recognized the private as one who had pulled a double shift and who was simply dead on his feet, undeserving of the insults heaped on him by the cocky major. Something in the way the kid bristled under the words "gold-bricking SOB" told me he was about to snap. Just as he pulled his hand back and bunched a fist, I grabbed him from behind and wrestled him to the floor. While sitting on the kid, I apologized to the major, telling him the private was in an irrational state due to lack of sleep and that I'd be responsible for getting him in shape. This appeased the officer with no further incident. A few days later, Colonel McKewen called me into his office.

"I heard what you did for that kid," he said without preamble.

"Yes sir," was all I could say.

"You know he would have probably faced a court martial if you hadn't stepped in."

"Yes sir."

"You did the right thing. I've been watching you, Jim. I need someone who can handle these officers. I'm putting you in charge of the officer's ward."

That took me by surprise. "Why?"

"I need someone who'll keep these guys in line. When they get here after their thirty missions, they're prone to a lot of temptation, mostly sneaking off base to be with their families. As of today, I want you to move in with them, keep an eye on them."

A baby-sitting job. I didn't recognize the order from McKewen as a sign of his trust in me, only as another damn responsibility. And one in which I was soon put to another test.

As the Colonel warned me, officers came to me weekly begging to be let off base for unauthorized conjugal visits. Most of the time, I okayed their unofficial leave with the condition that they return to their quarters by daylight. Though my reputation for taking the private to the floor may have influenced the success rate I had with unauthorized leaves returning as promised, I prefer to believe it was the fact that I always treated the enlisted men as equals. They left with the knowledge that I placed great trust in them and returned faithful to that trust.

My biggest problem was dealing with my conscience when facing the Colonel. After all, they were unauthorized leaves. Finally, one day over coffee, I couldn't stand it any longer.

"Colonel, I've got to confess something. I've been sizing these boys up. They're good kids, they've been risking their lives day in, day out; I've been letting them slip out to go home, but with the promise that they'll be back."

Whether it was the caffeine or just nervousness, I would have rattled on if the Colonel hadn't interrupted me. "I knew you were gonna do that, Jim."

"You did?"

"That's why I put you there—they weren't gonna let you down. Just like that kid you went to the floor with. You know when it's the right thing to do."

Not too long after this, the Colonel called me in and told me to drop my pants. He wanted to check me for a hernia. I don't think it even occurred to me to question the Colonel's sudden interest in my well-being. I figured he was looking for a patient to give the other doctors more practice on for this type of surgery, since many of the cadets would need such correction in order to withstand the g-force in flight.

The Colonel seemed delighted. "By God, you've got one. McSwain, get in here and fix this hernia," he called to one of my colleagues.

Within the hour, I was numbed by a spinal block but coherent and able to converse with my surgeon while the procedure took place. Harvard-trained, McSwain was originally from Arcadia, Florida—a man who was as comfortable performing a soft shoe as he was with a scalpel. A wonderful clown as I remember, though I wasn't in a position to evoke his comedic talents that day.

"Can you find the hernia?" I asked in what I thought was an humble voice.

"Shut up," he growled.

"It's on the anterior medial aspect of the cord," I offered.

"I know where it is," the Harvard man reminded me. After what seemed like five minutes, he announced, "All right, I guess we'll sew you up now."

"Be careful what you tie up down there," I had to wise off.

The scar left on my belly was my legacy from Colonel McKewen. Had he not ordered the hernia surgery, I would have been shipped to the South Pacific, I discovered much later. His confidence in me as well as a genuine liking prompted the idea of emergency surgery to keep me at SAACC while he sent another doctor in my place.

In the two years I spent under Colonel McKewen, I learned more than sound diagnostic and surgical techniques; the example he set in treating enlisted men and officers alike, affording them a sense of personal worth, taught me humility. His foresight in giving a rookie like me the freedom to do what I thought was right allowed me to develop that which no school can teach —a sense of ethics.

# CHAPTER XIII

# Cardinal Rule #3

If you are not circumcised, wash under the foreskin.

You would think that this is common sense for the uncircumcised male by the time he reaches adulthood. In my experience, however, good hygiene appears to be a learned behavior among humans, male or female.

After peace was declared in 1945, GI's were released gradually into civilian life, giving them time to make the most of what benefits they could while still in the employ of the U.S. Government. One of these benefits was free medical care, which translated to elective surgeries by the time many of them reached the states. As they came through the hospital at San Marcos Army Airfield, one of the most frequently requested surgeries was circumcision.

To label the average field conditions as unsanitary during wartime is an understatement. Under such conditions, uncircumcised soldiers suffered with constant infections due to bacteria trapped beneath the foreskin. Before returning home, these men not only sought treatment but were usually ready to do whatever was advised to prevent the situation from occurring again. For some, simply entering a lifestyle with access to adequate facilities and opportunity to bathe on a daily basis would put an end to these infections. For others, the lack of proper knowledge and training about personal hygiene during their formative years practically guaranteed further bouts of infection and/or more serious problems with the penis.

By this time, staff physicians at the base hospital were not only comfortable with performing circumcisions, but we had developed some pat, albeit callous replies when these men got up the courage to request the surgery. Typically, a doctor-patient consultation would proceed as follows:

Soldier: "Well, what do you do with that skin when you take it off?"

Doctor: "We save 'em up and make lampshades out of 'em."

A few GIs accepted this answer with the equanimity of a sheep in a shearing shed, but most responded with a snicker, then demanded to know what we really did with the foreskin.

This took some creativity on our part. "There's a tom cat that's been around the hospital for awhile now. Somehow, he's figured out when we're doing circumcisions. See that window over there that has no screen on it? When we're done we just pitch the foreskin out to him."

This usually solicited an outburst from the patient, if not a sudden change of mind about the procedure.

Far and away, the most popular retort to foreskin queries, which usually got a "Let 'er rip!" response, was "Oh, we send it to officer's candidate school and pin second lieutenant's bars on it."

# CHAPTER XIV

## Abortions

In the course of treating women for complications from abortions, the majority of them first-time patients, I gained a reputation that brought a number of patients to me requesting abortions. In post-World War II East Texas, the word abortion was not spoken in polite company and any doctor who wanted to build a respectable practice didn't perform an abortion without serious repercussions to his reputation in the medical community.

Small-town America always seems to be the last place to reflect a nation's discord or effort to embrace change. In the midst of the sixties revolution and the seventies resolutions (i.e., Supreme Court rulings) Nacogdoches maintained its quaint, introverted outlook. As issues of intense controversy and debate like the Vietnam War and Civil Rights dominated the front pages of newspapers from Washington, D.C., to Dallas, the news in Nacogdoches revolved around homecoming parades and cattle prices. While photos in *Life Magazine* dramatized protest marches for birth control and women's rights regarding unwanted pregnancies, such topics in Nacogdoches were relegated to carefully-worded pamphlets in churches or the environs of the protected doctor-patient relationship.

The conservative core of small towns like Nacogdoches often pressured an unwed pregnant woman into one of two courses of action: Abortion or immediate marriage to legitimize the baby. During the height of my practice, primarily the fifties through the seventies, Nacogdoches probably saw no more un-planned pregnancies than any other town of similar demo-graphics, even taking into account its fluctuating college popu-lation. However, few physicians would perform abortions, result-ing in back-alley practitioners.

In an era when the adulation of young girls made icons of actresses such as the perpetual ingenue Sandra Dee or the vir-ginal Doris Day, Nacogdoches saw a proliferation of back-street abortions, many of them performed by untrained attendants. The fear of discovery among their families and the community that they not only indulged in sex before marriage but became pregnant overshadowed any fear of physical pain involved in going through an abortion. Interruption of pregnancies by un-trained or medically-irresponsible attendants inevitably drew me into a controversial arena.

When a patient came to me requesting termination of preg-nancy, my first response was to suggest that she marry the father and keep the child. If the pregnancy was the result of a couple who were in love and had planned on marrying anyway, my advice was generally taken. I can honestly say that the resulting child of that union was usually the best child in every way. In my years of specializing in a field that strives to preserve the health of that well of procreation, the womb, I witnessed such a wide spectrum of circumstances affecting a woman's decision to go through abortion that I had to question my own philosophies and beliefs.

My internship at Parkland Hospital in Dallas included treatment of incomplete abortions and infections resulting from botched terminations. This training served me well for the patients that came to me under these circumstances and though I didn't condone abortion, I never turned away a patient that came to me as a result of complications.

One form of pregnancy intervention that I witnessed at Parkland was dilation and curettage, usually recommended for a patient who had been a rape or incest victim. This scraping of the lining of the uterus seems quite justifiable to me in the case of a woman whose life has already been altered tragically by the act of non-consensual sex. I question any reasoning that supports ruining the woman's life by forcing her to be reminded of a demoralizing act, which often results not only in an emotional burden but a financial one as well. A pregnancy thrust upon a woman under these circumstances robs her of dignity and self-esteem as she experiences not only months of intense physiological changes but the fear of raising a child with possible psychological or physical defects.

One of the few times I was ever called to testify against another physician in a lawsuit involved a doctor who regularly performed abortions in Nacogdoches. His patient, a young college student, was the daughter of close friends who called me to their home when she started vomiting, running a high fever and complaining of abdominal pain. At first I was inclined toward a diagnosis of infection, with no guess as to the source until more tests could be run. As I started her on an IV drip for fluid replacement and told her I'd like to conduct more tests at the hospital, she informed me of an abortion she'd had two days earlier. Emotionally, it was as painful a confession as I've ever witnessed. It also set off a number of alarms to me as the attending physician that I tried not to convey to the patient. With a stethoscope on her abdomen, I listened for the normal gurgling sounds of the gastrointestinal tract. Hearing nothing for several minutes, I knew she was in trouble.

After assuring her that everything would be all right, I left the room to tell her parents that we needed to get her to the hospital immediately for surgery. Inevitably, disclosure of her abortion came out. While it was obvious that the news devastated them, their foremost reaction was that whatever it took, their daughter's health could not be jeopardized. Their concern for her mental and physical well-being at that moment was as honest as any display of unconditional love I've known.

That day, with Dr. Larry Walker at my side, we ended up removing part of her small bowel and re attaching it to the large bowel, which was leaking through a hole punched through the uterine wall by an instrument used in the abortion procedure.

The patient came through the surgery and recovered within a few days, but not without great physical cost. Between the damage done by the abortion and the alterations made during corrective surgery, it was doubtful she'd ever conceive or have a child by natural means. Both she and the parents took this news hard. Within a couple of weeks they contacted me about testifying on her behalf if they brought a lawsuit for malpractice against the physician who performed the abortion. I admired her courage in facing the kind of exposure such a trial would bring about in her life. Though I despised the other physician for his lack of character in general, it was out of respect for her pursuit of righting a terrible wrong that I agreed to testify.

Just prior to our appointed court date, the abortion "specialist" visited me in my office. After a perfunctory greeting, he tried to coach me about the upcoming testimony. "Here's what you're going to say—" he started and got no further. I shook my head and gestured abruptly toward the exit. "No way," I said through clenched teeth, resisting the urge to knock him to the floor. He was smart enough to sense my rage and left without another word.

In the courtroom, I demonstrated the perforation of the uterine wall that caused the leakage of the bowel into the abdominal cavity by marking a life-size drawing for the jury in graphic detail. In my mind, the doctor who dealt such injury should have been charged with a criminal offense. Instead, he merely lost the suit to the family, was fined and left town soon after the trial. I learned later that he was practicing as usual in a larger city.

Perhaps the most insidious method of abortion I learned of when a patient came to me with an infected uterus involved the use of a branch from the slippery elm tree.

When the bark of a limb from this tree is peeled away, a smooth shiny surface is revealed, promoting a widespread belief among back-street attendants that the limb is sterile, having never been exposed to the air or soil. In the same manner in which coat-hanger abortions were performed, a branch about the diameter of a pencil was inserted in the woman's vagina and used to probe until the fetus was disturbed enough to become detached or die and later be sloughed. A virulent form of streptococcus is introduced into the uterus by this method of interruption, causing such severe infection that in a majority of cases, if not for antibiotics and intensive care, death would ensue.

In the end, the decision is the woman's. Sometimes the reasons for considering terminating a pregnancy were financially-driven, as in cases of families that expanded beyond the breadwinner's capacity to adequately feed and clothe them. Because I had witnessed a certain amount of neglect in large, poor families as well as a physical and/or mental breakdown in the mother of the children when the bulk of childrearing fell upon her, I often tried to talk my patients into letting me tie their tubes after their third delivery.

Whether the decision to terminate a pregnancy is spurred by an unplanned act of passion or a rape, that decision is ultimately within the power of the bearer of that child. No one can know the quandary of that person without stepping inside her mind and body.

A poet-writer I greatly admire for his insightful passages regarding marriage and children put it thus:

Your children are not your children.
They are the sons and daughters of Life's longing for itself.
They come through you but not from you,
And though they are with you yet, they belong not to you.

You may give them your love but not your thoughts,
For they have their own thoughts.
You may house their bodies but not their souls,
For their souls dwell in the house of tomorrow,
which you cannot visit, not even in your dreams.
You may strive to be like them, but seek not to make them
    like you.
For life goes not backward nor tarries with yesterday.

You are the bows from which your children as living arrows
    are sent forth.
The archer sees the mark upon the path of the infinite,
and He bends you with His might that His arrows may go
    swift and far.

Let your bending in the archer's hand be for gladness;
For even as He loves the arrow that flies,
so He loves also the bow that is stable.

—Kahlil Gibran

# CHAPTER XV

# Entrepreneur

Convinced that the bitter fruit from an East Texas hardwood tree was a natural roach repellent, a colleague of mine mailed some of these "horse apples" to a company that produced insecticides, hoping to cash in on the new formula.

This same entrepreneur talked me into attending a hypnosis workshop to add to our physician training, then tricked me into being one of the guinea pigs during the demonstration.

Ever the sucker for his enthusiastic, can't-fail attitude, I even agreed to let Eugene Rogers use my bald head in a hair-growing experiment.

Dr. Eugene Rogers and I met for the first time when I was stationed in San Marcos during the war. As chief of surgical services at the aviation training center, I supervised other physicians not only in medical procedures but in sanitary practices, which included preventive measures for combating malaria. My hands-on approach included a field trip to teach the new physicians about breeding sites for the malaria-carrying mosquito. In the back of the troop carrier that took us to a site with stagnant water, I sat next to a gregarious fellow from Minden, Louisiana. I never imagined we would one day be colleagues in the piney woods of East Texas.

Like many physicians after the war, Eugene Rogers wanted to go into private practice. Coincidentally, the small town of Garrison had a new clinic in need of a full-time physician. Though

Rogers specialized in internal medicine, he took the job because he liked what he saw; the terrain wasn't much different from his hometown and the population was growing. Our paths crossed socially and professionally during his short tenure in Garrison. After he fulfilled a second tour of duty in the Army during the early fifties, he returned to the area to jump-start his practice in Nacogdoches, where our careers took a parallel course.

Besides myself, Rogers was one of the few physicians in the county that was young enough to withstand the rigors of house-calls. Though we weren't partners, we often referred one another to patients and occasionally saw patients together. The importance of housecalls in those days can't be exaggerated—because of the isolation of some of these patients and scarcity of transportation, we never knew what we would find. In one case, the patient died before we arrived and the grief-stricken husband was moaning about "not wanting to go on without her," prompting a suicide watch. In such a case, the backup of a fellow physician was not only reassuring, but reinforcing.

No doubt, a housecall to one of those rough-sawed pine lumber houses on pier-and-beam inspired Rogers to market a "natural" insecticide. Probably the same old-timers that say pine needles in a dog house will repel fleas told him that rolling horse apples under your house would run roaches off. Horse apple is the common term for the fruit of the Osage-orange tree, a small hardwood that breaks the monotony of sweetgums and oaks in East Texas pastures and upland forests. When ripe, its nubby, baseball-size fruit drops to the ground. Inside an apple-green exterior, the core is hard and excretes a bitter, chalky fluid when pierced.

Only after he mailed several of the balls to a nationally-known roach spray manufacturer did Rogers let me in on his plan to profit from this discovery. Unfortunately, the company's laboratory reported that in their testing, roaches as well as silverfish and ants crawled all over the fruit with no apparent ill effects. No matter. When an idea didn't pan out, Rogers simply did what any prospector with gold fever would do: He moved on to another stream, sifting through countless clumps of mud and humus, believing that he would eventually find the precious metal.

In the spring of 1958, Rogers called me one day.

"There's a hypnosis convention coming to Houston. We need to go down there and get certified."

Chuckling, I took the bait. "What are we going to do with hypnosis?"

As usual, Rogers had heard just enough to put the wheels in motion. "We're going to use it on patients that don't respond to drugs. The possibilities are endless; no one else here does it."

I was curious enough about the process to agree to go with Rogers to the convention. Not that I really believed that it could work at that point, but it was a good time to take a trip and circulate with other physicians.

In the fifties, the Shamrock Hotel in Houston attracted guests as varied as sports celebrities and oil magnates and hosted conventions in an atmosphere of charm and elegance. Its reputation probably accounted for the standing-room-only crowd at the hypnosis convention. Rogers and I arrived late and shortly after we were seated, a psychiatrist named Erickson from Arizona called for a volunteer.

Rogers nudged me. "Let's see if he can really put someone under," he whispered and gestured toward the aisle in such a way that I assumed we were both volunteering.

Since I was closest to the end of the row, I got up, expecting him to follow, only to realize when I turned around that I'd been had. Rogers remained in his seat and the audience eyed me expectantly as Dr. Erickson thanked me for volunteering.

The psychiatrist's piercing blue eyes took in my sunburned forearm, prompting him to guess that I might have been fishing recently. I have to wonder what scenario he would have introduced for me in the hypnosis demonstration if he'd known I got the sunburn from propping my arm out the window on the drive to Houston.

His voice low and soothing, Erickson prompted me to close my eyes and drift into a sleep-like state. Telling me I was at a lake, he had me casting for and catching imaginary fish before the audience of physicians. How many in the room knew that I was pretending I'll never know, but seeing no point in embarrassing Erickson or my colleagues, I followed his suggestions throughout the demonstration. Rogers was convinced I had been put under. Figuring I could wait until after the convention to enlighten him, I returned to my seat prepared to view the remainder of the convention with great cynicism.

The next volunteer was a young woman from Austin. I watched her closely, wondering if she would fake it as I had. To my amazement, it was obvious that she was truly reliving her past at Erickson's prompting, going back to her first grade class and rattling off the names of all of her classmates. Such a range of emotion passed through the young physician before Erickson brought her out of the trance that I was convinced the greatest actress in the world couldn't have pulled off a better performance. No, this was real.

Rogers and I returned to Nacogdoches with certificates in hand, stating that the participant in Seminars on Hypnosis ". . . completed a course of instruction and practice in Induction Procedures, Hypnotheraphy, and Hypnodontics," signed and dated May 11, 1958 by Erickson and a team of specialists.

I used hypnosis rarely, but not because of skepticism. On the contrary, patients I hypnotized successfully came out the suggestive state so relaxed and at peace that they wanted to return often for a treatment they didn't need. My concern was their psychological dependence on me in an area in which I felt I had no real expertise.

This decision was reinforced by an incident that occurred in the office I shared with Dr. Walter B. Allen. Like me, Allen scoffed at the field of hypnosis as viable medical treatment but couldn't quell a curiosity about the technique, especially after Rogers and I returned from the Houston convention. One night over dinner at a supper club he asked me if I thought I could actually induce hypnosis. With little preamble, I talked him into a state of suggestion and asked him some things about his past. After a few minutes I brought him out of the trance and told him what he had said. When he realized that I couldn't have obtained the information any other way, his skepticism dissolved. The longer he thought about it, the more enticing the idea became. All he could think about was applying the technique to one of his patients.

At Allen's insistence, I coached him on approach and follow-through until he felt he could perform hypnosis on his own. On a day that I was seeing patients at the office, the door to

Allen's examination room flew open and a barrel-shaped woman bustled out, exclaiming "Dr. Allen, what are you doin' to me?" She left the clinic without further explanation, the object of great curiosity among a waiting room full of patients.

Allen immediately came to me wanting to know what he had done wrong. The woman had agreed to try hypnosis to overcome a weight problem, but wasn't responding to Allen's voice. Instead of admitting that it wasn't working with her, he repeated instructions to the point that he alarmed her to his inexperience. Fortunately, the incident seemed to have no lasting repercussions, other than Allen opting to never try hypnotism again.

Horse apples. Hypnosis. What was Rogers going to get me into next?

Hair.

The catalyst for the hair experiment was a casual remark thrown out by a friend over coffee one day. Robert Griffin had 600 acres of the sweetest pasture just outside the city limits. I always enjoyed visiting with Griffin because his experiences reminded me of many of the farmers I came to know and like as a teenager working for my Dad at the flour mill in Denton.

Our conversation had shifted to receding hairlines.

"I'd give my farm to grow hair on my head!" Griffin exclaimed loud enough for most of the customers around us to hear.

Rogers was one of those customers. Later, he cornered me and asked if I thought Griffin was serious.

"Sure enough," I said, half-joking.

That and a guinea pig named Jim Taylor were all the encouragement Rogers needed to proceed with the hair experiment. Inspired by the stimulating properties of a new drug on the market, Rogers formulated a treatment using cortisone injections to induce hair growth on the scalp. My scalp, to be precise.

With the 600 acres dangling in front of us like a carrot, Rogers talked me into letting him inject the drug intradermally into the tender hide on my head, which had been hairless for several years.

Meanwhile, we had a third party interested in the wager. Dr.

L. W. "Legs" Snider, Rogers' successor at the Garrison clinic, acted as an observer and occasional advisor in the experiment. The three of us met four times the first week, conferring in a room at the back of Robertson's Pharmacy, where we could conduct the experiment with some degree of privacy while waiting for positive results.

After three treatments, the cortisone injections yielded no sign of follicle development. All I had to show for the excruciating pricks on my cueball head was a pattern of red welts, too-precisely placed to explain away as bee stings. Rogers and Snider discussed changes in the dosage of the active ingredient, which might have been enough encouragement for me continue in my role as lab rat if they hadn't started chuckling every time they stuck me. By the end of the second week, I told them to find a new rat.

For Rogers, another foray into the entrepreneurial side of medicine came to an abrupt end. For three young physicians, a friendship was forged, strengthened in years to follow by the retelling of just such a foray.

Eugene Rogers died on a December day in 1995, losing a valiant battle to cancer. When I hear about innovative medical procedures or new miracle drugs today, I often speculate about the call I'd be getting from my gregarious friend from Louisiana if he were still here. Sign me up, Rogers.

# CHAPTER XVI

# Philosophers

By the end of my first year of private practice in Nacogdoches, I knew every major farm-to-market road in three counties and people knew my car. As my patient list grew, I like to think it was because I was young and wanted to make a good impression, but more likely it was because I would make housecalls virtually anywhere and anytime. People also knew if they could catch up with my car, they'd have as good a chance at getting medical attention as they would in the hospital emergency room or the office I rented downtown.

It was easier for a bootlegger to hide whiskey at a church revival than it was for me to elude total strangers seeking medical treatment.

Not only did people try to catch up to me when they spied my '46 Ford Coupe in the hospital parking lot, they waited half a day in the drugstore on the gamble that I'd be coming by sooner or later. This played havoc on those waiting for me back at the office. I'd listen to congested babies, look into an infected ear, or maybe diagnose and treat a case of gout before I left the drugstore "waiting room." Delays caused by the drugstore patients were so frequent that the pharmacist felt sorry for me and started keeping a sandwich for me under the counter.

Occasionally the recipients of these unscheduled consultations would offer to pay me the customary office fee of three dollars, but times were hard and more often they simply thanked me. I didn't let them go without writing down instructions, a sound bit of advice I'd been given by a nurse during my internship at Parkland. She cautioned me that the majority of patients don't remember verbal instructions by the time they get home. Almost without exception, I found that when I asked them to repeat the instructions back to me, they left out a step or got numbers wrong, whether it had to do with times of day for treatment or the amount of medication to take. If I had to use the glasstop counter at the drugstore or the gleaming metal hood of my car, it didn't matter. I found it worth the time to write down instructions for those random patients.

I truly love healing. Most of the time, I welcomed the chance to help, no matter how much it stretched the day. Some days, I completely lost track of time, not realizing what time of day it was until I stepped outside, looked toward Douglass and couldn't see the sun, only the tinted sky above timberline. Dusk. To East Texans, the sun seems to take its sweet time setting, probably because we can never see it claimed by the horizon. The fading light subtly reminded me I needed to start home if I wanted to see the kids before they went to bed.

As Sarah and I would catch up on our day over a late, warmed-up meal and I'd entertain thoughts of going to that big chair in the living room and reading before bed, it would happen.

A knock at the back door. Sometimes a honk from the driveway. They knew where I lived, these strangers I'd never seen but who couldn't wait until the following day to come to see me at the office.

Even for a man of my motivation and vigor, the growing consistency of this type of interruption was wearing me down. One day I vented my frustration to an older, established physician in the area. His advice, delivered with the dryness of a shallow well drawn from by one-too-many generations, gave me my first taste of East Texas philosophy.

"If you don't want people to come to your back door at night, you've got to do two things: Get naked and drunk. Works every time—when they see you like that, they won't chance another visit to your home."

I didn't doubt that this was solid advice, the kind that had been put to the test by that particular physician. Nevertheless, it was advice I only passed along for what it was worth. Had I used it, I'm sure life would have been easier in some respects. Certainly interesting.

But then I wouldn't have met people like the elderly rail of a man that came out to my house one evening, years after I'd retired, because he heard that Dr. Taylor would treat you regardless if you could pay. Or had the chance to reminisce about a former patient when her son stopped by, dripping blood on my doorstep, because my house was closer than the hospital.

An accident with a hand tool, he said.

Don't know if I have anything here to sew it up with, I told him.

Don't care if it's quiltin' thread, Dr. Taylor, he countered. I don't have insurance. Can you help me?

Saved from a dull evening of reading a medical journal.

One of the most original of East Texas philosophers I knew during the early years of my practice was Doc Parmley. He wasn't a physician. Doc worked with his hands, building roads before the days of gasoline-powered backhoes and graders. In my mind, a man who could work this road base of red clay with mules and scoops probably had as much or more to say about life than any physician. Near the end of his life, I was Doc's attending physician.

Doc knew that he was dying. One of the last times I saw him as a patient was during the dog days of summer. Somehow the scalding August heat amplified the sense of desperation I felt at witnessing the stage of suffering under which traditional medication—i.e. pain-killing injections, i.v. sedation, etc.—has become ineffectual. Partly because I was at a loss for words to comfort such a proud man and partly because I knew that one in such an humbling situation appreciates any distraction, I asked him if he had any sage advice to pass on.

On the subject of marriage, Doc felt unusually qualified.

"You don't know a woman 'til you've wintered with her. In summer, she can walk down in the pasture, get away from you if things ain't goin' right. In winter, you're closed up together. Mistake I made was never wintering with a woman before I married her."

Doc was married seven times.

The subject of marriage, particularly when it came to why or when people should consider it, inspired a would-be philosopher I knew only as the Lamp-post Man. During the years I kept an office downtown above the Swift Brothers and Smith Pharmacy, I greeted acquaintances and strangers alike throughout the day, usually with a nod, sometimes stopping long enough to comment on the weather or inquire about their health. It wasn't uncommon to see a man leaning against one of the Victorian-style natural gas lamps that lined the brick streets.

There was nothing extraordinary about the Lamp-post Man. He wasn't young or old. He wore a clean suit and tipped his hat to the ladies. His occupation was suspect; he seemed to have a lot of time for observing people. Like most of the East Texas philosophers I've met, he spoke with the simplicity of a white-bread recipe that leaves a curiously "wry" aftertaste:

"I've never seen a man marry a man or woman marry a woman. If it weren't for a man and woman, there'd be very little marrying done."

# CHAPTER XVII

# Cardinal Rule #4

Dr. A. A. Nelson, a beloved physician who practiced in Nacogdoches before my time, dispensed medical advice like General Patton counseled troops. He was as direct with female patients as he was with male patients, as a young woman with questionable hygiene habits who came to his office discovered one day.

Without preamble, Dr. Nelson said, "You have an odor about you. You need to bathe."

"Doctor, I do bathe. I wash up as far as possible and I wash down as far as possible."

"Well, wash Possible," Nelson countered, providing those of us that came to treat the "unwashed" of Nacogdoches years later with a frame of reference never to be forgotten.

Proper hygiene continued to be a significant issue between patients and physicians of the generation that followed Dr. Nelson's. The advent of radio and television advertisement, particularly regarding feminine cleanliness, helped awaken a lot of women to a new level of personal hygiene. Occasionally, such ads caused a good intention to backfire, as in the case of perfumed douches.

When attending a patient in the capacity of her gynecologist, I usually recommended she avoid perfumed douches, to cut down on allergic reactions within the ultra-sensitive dermis of the vaginal area.

94

The most effective formula I can recommend to women for cleansing and refreshing that part of the female anatomy that is incomparable as a breeding ground for bacteria is what their mothers and grandmothers relied upon: A half cup of vinegar to a large douche bag, once or twice a week.

Of equal importance in guarding against irritations and infections is the choice of underwear; always wear cotton. Women living in the semi-tropical climate of East Texas are especially susceptible to the irritations that result from wearing garments that don't "breathe." For the same reason you wouldn't wear nylon socks to jog in a 10-K marathon, you want to avoid nylon against the crotch.

*Dr. William W. Henderson, friend and internist who has guided the author through recent years with unparalleled excellence in medical care.*

# Chapter XVIII

# Humor the Patient

Whether it's securing investors or selling the latest model Lincoln Continentals to die-hard Chevy customers, bankers and automobile dealers alike recognize that successful interaction calls for flexibility in accommodating the needs of the client. This same type of flexibility promotes successful interaction between doctors and their patients. At times, it may require a compromise of one's personal or professional bias. In the business world, humoring the client can be the psychological edge that clinches a deal. In the medical profession, humoring the patient can be the physician's edge in eliciting cooperation and trust.

During my tenure at the 150-bed hospital at San Marcos Army Airfield in the forties, we approached many of our patients with a sense of humor which lacked the finer art of compromise.

Besides circumcision, a frequently-requested elective procedure at the airfield was hemorrhoid removal. Though surgical procedure was usually the 'last resort' method of treatment for hemorrhoids, particularly in young patients, efforts to convince the soldiers this was not in their best interest were not well met. They saw the surgery as immediate eradication of a grievous condition. That's when we turned them over to the scrub nurse, a man named Frietag, who was as sympathetic as a country cur is to the UPS driver. We could always rely on Sgt. Frietag to dissuade those that insisted on the surgery.

"There's another one out here that wants hemorrhoids removed, Doc," Frietag would announce. "I'll go and get the chair."

The patient usually took the bait. "What's the chair for?"

Without hesitation Sgt. Frietag answered, "We've got this old wicker chair with the bottom out of it and to save time, we just let you sit there and cut off whatever hangs through."

Most of the soldiers in the waiting room exited upon hearing this, no matter what their reason for being there.

With its strict chain of command and narrow scope of patients, the military environment only half-prepared me for my post-war entrance into the private sector, or more accurately the rural sector, particularly when it came to humoring the patient. In the army, keeping an open-door relationship with other physicians helped me hone this tool more than interaction with patients. Later, in private practice, I found that people in general and especially East Texans were most responsive to treatment once I adopted a less traditional approach and humored them.

At City Memorial Hospital, the staff was accustomed to a certain amount of compromise with patients after they were admitted, which would typically involve food smuggled in for them by visitors or a clothing substitute for the dreaded hospital gown. The spirit of compromise ran head-on into another kind of spirit the evening we tried to admit an alcoholic that wouldn't part with his bottle.

Early diagnosis indicated the man had pneumonia, which had not progressed beyond a stage easily treatable. The problem developed when we explained the treatment to the patient, which would require a two-to-three-day hospital stay while we administered expectorants and penicillin. When one of the nurses told him he'd have to forego the whiskey while he stayed in our "hotel," he held the bottle closer to him and explained that he couldn't go through treatment without a nip every now and then.

The nurse gamely offered to keep the bottle under lock and key for him until he was released, triggering a glowering look and shake of the head from the man. I could see that he was considering walking out and rather than let him leave with a high probability of not recovering, I began the deal-making.

"If you'll go quietly with the nurse," I urged, "you can have a sip when you get to the room. Then we'll talk about a schedule of treatment."

I could feel the eyes of the staff boring into me, wondering about this new kind of treatment.

After he'd had a chance to settle in the room, I went to him and explained that we wouldn't cut him off from the whiskey entirely but that we needed to keep it in a safer place than his room, due to the number of visitors on the floor every day. He couldn't argue that his room wasn't very private—his bed was in a ward—but he did show me and the staff an unexpected turn of compromise.

Stepping out in the middle of the hall for the most effect, he held up the bottle for everyone to see and proclaimed that he would make sure no one else sampled from his bottle. He then spit in it and handed it over to the nurse.

During his three-day stay, the patient responded well to the treatment, with no adverse side effects in spite of his whiskey allowance, doled out to him several times daily. Though I hoped the compromise wouldn't set a precedent among alcoholic patients, I didn't regret following my instincts with that patient.

I had no worries about setting a precedent, however, with accommodating the wishes of one particular obstetrics patient.

After delivering a healthy boy baby, the woman I attended insisted that I inscribe the birth certificate with the name "Pislum Siv." Assuming some connection to a family name, I didn't say anything, though I'm sure my expression conveyed curiosity to say the least.

After I signed the certificate she told me to hand her a dog-eared Bible she'd brought with her to the hospital. Flipping it open with a tattered silk ribbon, she pointed to "Psalms CIV." She could barely read but had memorized several passages and arrived at the peculiar pronunciation apparently on her own.

I left the name spelled on the birth certificate precisely as she pronounced it.

Humoring the patient often extends to the patient's family. In the course of losing a patient, Dr. Eugene Rogers and I came upon a treatment for depression that we coined the Tippet Treatment. Mrs. Tippet, a middle-aged woman who suffered from extreme hypertension, was obese to the extent that when she lay in a hospital bed, rolls of flesh mounded beneath the white sheets so that you couldn't have fit a pencil in the bed next to her.

The Tippets lived in a small cabin where chickens wandered in and out, as the door had to be left open to help fan her bed. Mr. Tippet had purchased a custom-made bed to accommodate his wife's great girth and in the last year of her bedridden life, he left her side only under great duress. Shortness of breath plagued her for some time but when her heart gave out suddenly, her husband wasn't prepared.

Before daylight one summer morning, my phone rang.

"My wife died last night," Mr. Tippet blurted out. His voice broke, the raw emotion in it reminding me of a shipwrecked passenger that reaches the safety of a lifeboat only to turn and watch loved ones not so lucky slip beneath the waves. "I think I'll take a pistol to my head and shoot myself."

After trying to console him for several minutes with no sign of his suicidal reaction subsiding, I told him I'd be over right away with Dr. Rogers. Though my gut feeling told me he was more incoherent with grief than suicidal, I felt safer with another doctor in tow. I'd learned to take nothing for granted when it came to housecalls.

The scenarios that played in our minds on the drive out to the Tippets' probably aged Rogers and me ten years. We didn't have to speak to know what the other was thinking. Simultaneous relief flooded over us when we came upon the Tippet house, its modest seams bulging with good-hearted neighbors attempting to console the widower.

We tried to convince the grieving husband that the extraordinary care he'd given his wife had without question extended her life much longer than was warranted for someone in her condition. Mr. Tippet remained inconsolable, wringing his hands and sobbing pitifully.

We offered him a mild sedative but of course, he refused. As we started to leave, I approached the hovering group of neighbors.

"You know, if one of you could stay with him tonight, listen to his breathing, and just console him, maybe he can get through this."

No one said a word. Finally, a petite widow that lived a piece down the road spoke up, her meek stammer overcome by compassion. "I'll stay with . . . this fella and . . . listen to him and console him."

The next morning, again around daybreak, my phone rang.

"I feel great," a man's voice gushed. "I want you to know, the sky is blue, the grass is green, it's a wonderful world, and God's in his Heaven." His words and tone suffused with optimism, it was hard to believe that the caller was the same man I'd left twelve hours earlier.

Mr. Tippet later married the widow who stayed to console him. Whether directed toward patients or their families, Rogers and I derived great satisfaction in the prescribing of the Tippet Treatment, which amounted to no more than tender loving care.

When I was getting my practice off the ground, many established physicians in East Texas offered the benefit of their experience freely to me. Colorfully wrapped in the guise of anecdotal encounters with various characters and ailments, nonetheless it was advice I took to heart.

On the subject of humoring the patient, one physician's experience ranks above all others. His patient, a young woman of singular mind, suffered from chronic abdominal pain. Resistant to the doctor's suggestion that she undergo some tests in the hospital, she was determined to diagnose herself. She repeatedly told the doctor she was convinced she was carrying a parasite in her intestine. During the ensuing discussion of parasites known to thrive in the food chain of our warm, moist climate, she focused on and became obsessed with the notion that it wasn't a worm but a snake that was living in her large intestine.

The doctor approached treatment cautiously, until he could learn more about the patient's habits, if not mental acuity. A few days after hearing her emphatic self-diagnosis, this doctor took a day off for some fishing. While standing on the bank of a pond, he noticed a small green snake sunning itself. Pocketing the non-poisonous snake, he took it back to the hospital, where the woman had been admitted for observation.

After giving the obsessive patient a common laxative, he explained that the "medicine" she was taking would help her to pass the parasite. He then took a nurse into his confidence, explaining the idea behind his treatment and left the nurse to attend to the patient with a bed pan. The nurse followed the plan with no hitches, depositing a lifeless green snake in the bed pan when the moment was right.

The woman's delight in discovering that she had gotten rid of the "parasite" while proving to the medical community that her diagnosis was correct spilled over into effusive praise for her doctor. Coincidentally, her symptoms disappeared.

If I learned anything about earning a patient's trust and thereby executing a treatment under optimum conditions, it was the importance of not only hearing, but listening.

Judge Jack Pierce asked me to come over to the courthouse one day to evaluate the mental status of a man waiting in his office. Though I can't recall the man's name or the relevance of his presence before the judge, I do remember his response to a line of questioning I'd been trained to use in such situations.

I questioned him succinctly. "Is anyone after you?"

"No."

"Are you afraid enough to feel the need of killing a person?"

"No."

"Do you hear voices?"

"No."

"Do you hear things you are unable to see?"

"Yep."

I paused and asked him quietly, "What do you think they are?"

"Mosquitoes," he answered.

My evaluation for the judge was just as concise. "Judge, in my opinion, this man is normal, and smarter than I am."

The tendency among East Texans to speak simply and to the point, particularly those whose livelihood was agrarian in nature, was a characteristic I enjoyed the more I was around it.

One evening well after dark I was called to attend a patient admitted to the emergency room with some peculiar lacerations. As I entered the exam room, I was met by a man in his thirties with the weather-beaten face and callused hands of the quintessential 'rugged individual' who'd spent most of his life in the elements. The most immediate indication of his distress was his stage of undress: He wore a long nightshirt half-stuffed into pants that he clutched unfastened around his midsection. Whatever had prompted this hospital visit must have had an acute onset; in my experience up to that point, men of his generation would not have been seen away from home in their nightshirt, unless they were drunk or feeble-minded. This man appeared to be neither.

He said that he wanted me and only me to examine him. Though his wife had driven him to the hospital, she remained outside in the car. For the first few minutes of our patient-doctor consultation, he spoke in monosyllables punctuated by groans and gasps. This, along with his bowed stance and grimace told me that his pain probably emanated from the groin. I told him to drop his pants and let me take a look.

He hesitated before he complied, as much from embarrassment as from the pain of anything touching him in the area of injury. What I saw didn't enlighten me as to what kind of injury I was treating. The man's scrotum was criss-crossed with lacerations that looked like the work of a serrated knife blade.

As I scoured the room for the best cleaning agents possible, the peach farmer told his tale.

He'd just finished a late supper, was sitting around in his nightshirt, and decided to go for a walk to cool off. Before air-conditioning and the lure of television, it wasn't uncommon for people, especially those that lived in the country, to take a walk after dark during the peak months of the furnace called a Texas summer.

Stepping into some pants, he told his wife he was 'taking some air' in the orchard. Several hundred yards from the house his sphincter muscle told him he'd better look around for some leaves. It was a mild night and this was no great inconvenience, but he was thankful that no one could see him. He had failed to notice the playful kitten that followed him out to the orchard. As the farmer squatted beneath the low-slung branches of a peach tree, the kitten assumed a stalking pose.

Perhaps the kitten thought the man was teasing him by dangling two bulbous pouches just off the ground in the starlight. The farmer, however, was totally unaware of the kitten until he felt the fire of pouncing claws grab his testicles.

With the kitten attached firmly to its prize, the man ran

toward the house, making poor progress in the trailing pants, but yelling for his wife all the way. As he described the scene, the farmer's monosyllables spilled into more colorful language, his tongue no doubt loosened by the pain medication I'd given him.

I took great care in cleaning the wounds; cat scratch fever was as much a danger as infection. After suturing what I could, I gave him a tetanus shot and sent him on his way, reminding him to get an antibiotic prescription filled.

By the time I got to bed that night, I should have been too tired to think, but I couldn't get the image out of my head: Here was this strapping farmer, humbled first by the inconvenient timing of a bowel movement, then by a kitten's "attack." However, these events were overshadowed by his wife's lack of understanding about the precarious situation he was in and subsequent mishandling.

I would never forget the great tears welling in his eyes. An onlooker would have attributed them to the aggressive suturing I was applying to his genitalia at the time, but I sensed his anguish resulted from something more than physical pain.

When I asked him how the kitten came to inflict such wounds, I gained some insight into the true source of his pain, owing more to an internal wound—a sense of betrayal from his spouse—than from the external wounds.

"I told the wife 'Choke him off, honey, don't pull him off,' " he confided with great reluctance. Then, his head bowed, he moaned "She didn't pay me no mind."

# CHAPTER XIX

# A Physician's Reach

In the northernmost part of Nacogdoches County lies a community known as North Redland. Scarcely ten miles from the outer loop around the City of Nacogdoches, the beauty of the landscape, mostly prime pasture bordered by strips of majestic hardwoods, invites development. Yet, it is one of the few communities that has resisted subdivisions, remaining in the hands of many of the families I met there fifty years ago.

Other than some freshly-topped asphalt roads and bright green county road signs, the land remains as well-tended yet rural as it was when I made my first housecall there in 1946. A predominantly black community, North Redland produced some of the finest vegetables and melons to be found at the farmer's market. The land's fertility may have been due to some geological advantage, such as a variation of soils that allowed it to flourish despite erratic rainfall, late freezes, grasshopper swarms and the countless other obstacles East Texas farmers face. I lack any true agricultural experience to back such an observation; my hypothesis about the reason for this area's productivity is based purely on the experience of a city doctor making housecalls treating the people who worked this land. Consequently, I believe that the land's fertility is intertwined with the people who make their living from it.

Ironically, the land's unforgiving nature, specifically its unyielding mass, gave me opportunity to meet the people that broke its sod. My first housecall to North Redland involved treating a man who'd fallen from his horse.

A veritable patriarch of the community, Ned Johnson exemplified the character that permeated North Redland. Though he must have been in his sixties at the time, he had the physical strength and endurance of a man twenty years younger. This, along with the fact that he was a strikingly handsome black man with blue eyes, impressed most who met him for the first time. Even more impressive to me, however, was his presence of mind in directing his family to get help immediately after his fall. Suspecting that the numbness he felt from his neck down could get worse with the wrong movement, Mr. Johnson waited patiently on his back in the hot summer sun until I arrived, attended by his wife, a daughter and some nephews.

As anyone who is self-employed will attest, there comes a time when you wonder if the acquisition of certain equipment is a wise investment, particularly when first starting a practice. The purchase of a portable x-ray machine that fit in the trunk of my car invited such contemplation, especially in the beginning when I had an office to furnish and more than myself on the payroll. The Keleket portable x-ray paid for itself many times over that day, indicating that Mr. Johnson had indeed suffered injury to his fifth and sixth cervical vertebrae, putting pressure on nerves that affected the feeling in most of his body. To offset the damage, I explained, the best treatment would mean putting him in traction. Given the distance involved, condition of the roads, and type of ambulance available, I knew that the logistics of transporting him to the hospital for such treatment would dramatically increase his chance of permanent paralysis. We would have to set up something in his house, I reasoned.

After stabilizing his neck, I turned to the hovering family. Though Mr. Johnson spoke to them and appeared to be in no pain, they seemed to understand by my tone of voice and choice of words the gravity of his situation. After outlining a plan for moving him to the house, I had to say little else to galvanize the Johnson clan into action. Nephews with corded necks and biceps lifted him while his wife and daughter led the way. I marveled at the graceful precision with which they responded to a traumatic situation, affirming each other's moves quietly and instinctively.

After surveying the room where they deposited Mr. Johnson, I mentally clicked off the list of supplies I would need to rig him up for traction. Can someone dig up about five pounds of sand and bring it here in a bucket? I asked. One of the boys disappeared. To the daughter, who happened to be a registered nurse, I explained that I'd have to go to the hospital to get some traction equipment.

Later that day I returned with the special chin harness, pulley and rope.

For sheer effectiveness, the device we rigged for Mr. Johnson rivaled any we could have set up for him at the hospital, the main difference being the use of a bucket of sand rather than conventional weights for exerting the necessary pressure on his neck to correct the slipped vertebra. For six weeks, Mr. Johnson remained faithfully tied to this device, sleeping with the aid of a sedative I left for him. Every three or four days, I would come by to x-ray him and add or remove sand from the bucket, depending upon the progress of the displaced vertebra. Meanwhile, another daughter who worked as an R.N. in Houston came home to help. Between the moral and physical support of his family and the makeshift traction, Mr. Johnson recovered fully.

The success of Mr. Johnson's treatment cemented my reputation among the people of North Redland. Most of them, having never witnessed anyone in traction prior to this incident, probably thought I had invented it for that patient. Though I was gaining insight and professional maturity daily, many years passed before I realized the value of my internship at Parkland, where among other things, attending patients who required traction for conditions varying from congenital defects to sports-related accidents gave us an incredible grounding in the basics of applying this type of treatment.

Beyond knowledge, beyond physical skill, a physician has to reach within some aspect of himself when dealing with scenarios and environments not covered in medical school. Adaptability and improvisation are essential where equipment, personnel, or facilities are lacking.

And then there are cases when I believe a good physician can only step back in awe of what nature has done and relinquish all claim to the cure. In the case of an anomaly I dubbed the "blind pouch," I earned the gratitude of more than one couple who thought they couldn't have children. The "cure" simply entailed informing the patient of a rare physical anomaly that any physician who examined her thoroughly would have discovered, that she had two congenital vaginas, one that reached the cervix and one that didn't.

How lucky I felt to be able to deliver news a patient liked to hear—that conception was certainly realizable in spite of the blind pouch. Amazingly, I counseled three patients with this same anomaly during my practice. Once so informed, the patients simply applied their newfound knowledge of their bodies to the best advantage when trying to conceive.

There is no compensation in the profession, as far as I am concerned, that compares with the feeling I got when I could restore hope in a patient, particularly when that hope involved one of the greatest blessings in life, the ability to bear a child.

Inevitably there are the cases that come before all physicians that challenge our belief that, with the timely application of medicines and techniques modern science has put at our disposal, we can cheat death. Whether at the dawn of our careers, before inflated egos have been truly tested by the needle-prick of life experience, or the twilight of a practice, when knowledge of the power given us through the prescription of "miracle" drugs is equally as seductive as ego, we are vulnerable to the trap of thinking that at some point in a patient's life, we are omnipotent.

My awakening from this trap came in the form of a car accident victim brought to Memorial Hospital's emergency room in the fifties. A call came in that a seventeen-year-old male was being brought by ambulance from the scene of an accident that occurred in Diboll. Soon after his arrival to E.R., I was able to determine that his injuries weren't restricted to external bruising and lacerations. Between information from the Diboll doctor who had examined him just after the accident and his rapidly deteriorating vital signs, I deduced his spleen had ruptured. Despite the protection afforded this organ by its positioning in the human body, its sheath of papyrus-thin tissue makes it extremely vulnerable when a blow is delivered to the ribs. I made the decision to operate immediately.

While the medical team administered oxygen and blood

transfusions to the wraith-like figure, I wondered if we'd gotten him to surgery in time to save him. His vital signs held as I went about the removal of the now useless spleen, the source of his life-draining internal bleeding.

As he regained consciousness in recovery, he looked around the room with uncommon intensity, drawing me closer to his bedside.

His voice devoid of the hoarseness anesthesia often produces, he spoke with amazing clarity. "You know I was floatin' up there above you guys when you were workin' on me," he said for everyone's benefit, though his eyes locked with mine. As near death as he was upon arrival at the hospital, I don't know how he could have known I was the physician who examined him and ultimately operated on him.

His words tumbled out but his meaning was clear. "I wanted to say to you, leave me alone—I feel so good. I never felt this way on earth."

We had more than one discussion about his out-of-body experience before he left the hospital. When he told me later that he'd never fear death the way he did before the accident, I knew it wasn't the braggadocio of the typical teen, particularly boys who think death only happens to their grandparents. The euphoria he described must have occurred while his vital signs validated the state of deep shock I first observed him to be in. As he described the team and equipment used to resuscitate him at a moment I recalled all too vividly, as I was one of that team, it gave me something to ponder and relate to physicians with similar patients over the next thirty years: Despite our undeniable role on earth as an intelligent, evolving species, we must nevertheless yield to higher, yet more powerful forces when it comes to understanding the bridge between life and death.

# Chapter XX

# Cardinal Rule #5

Learn to pray.

I've prayed for many things in this life: A pony when I was a boy, the latest model Lincoln at almost every stage of my adult life, and once, for a dying man to live through the night so that people would not think me a murderer. And, like all medical students, at one point or another I prayed that I would pass an exam.

Sometime after college, however, prayer asserted itself in my life as naturally as the study of medicine had years earlier. I am my father's son in many ways, but I did not inherit his gift for invention. I've wondered at times, had I had been as gifted in my field as he was mechanically, where I'd be today if I had followed the paths of some of the more brilliant surgeons I know and devoted more to research. Could I have been of more service to my fellow man in a laboratory?

My approach to medicine has always been tempered by something outside the milieu of beakers, formulas, and 300-page tomes on the life-cycle of a particular bacteria. Interaction with the patient has always been a driving force in my life. When I could relieve a patient's suffering using the best approach science had to offer, I felt omnipotent. When all avenues of this approach were exhausted and I had to watch a patient slip away, I felt helpless until at some point, I learned to pray.

To some, the field of medicine is all-powerful when put to

*Nacogdoches Memorial Hospital, c. 1999*

its optimum use. Yet those who believe this will shake their heads fifty years from now as they reflect on the technological hurdles they had to overcome. If they live long enough, they will realize how little we actually know and how much we have yet to discover.

# Chapter XXI

# A Physician's Nightmare

From the beginning of my training as a physician, I never worried about protocol when it came to doing what I thought was right. Hesitation based on political correctness seemed pointless to me, especially when the time governing a course of action was critical to a patient's progress, if not survival. Doing the job the best way I knew how was paramount to me. At times, I'm sure my actions invited comparison to the proverbial fool that rushes in where angels fear to tread; when my instinct told me that what I did was best for the patient, I always thought the politics of the situation would resolve itself. It took me a long time to realize that nothing resolves itself.

As a physician, the first time I acted with reckless disregard for my own welfare was when I operated on an enlisted man's dependent at a facility designated for army personnel only. It was a quiet Saturday afternoon at the Army airfield hospital in San Marcos. A sergeant brought his seriously ill son to me because the nearest hospital for dependents was in San Antonio and he was worried about his boy's fever worsening during the drive. My first year at the San Marcos airfield hospital one of the most frequent problems I diagnosed and performed surgery for was appendicitis. I recognized the symptoms in the sergeant's son almost immediately. Certain that the boy's life would be in danger if delayed by the trip to San Antonio, I told his father we needed to operate immediately.

111

The sergeant was aware of the risk I was taking. If my C.O. found out I was operating on civilian personnel—even a soldier's dependent—I could be brought up on serious charges, if not shipped out to the farthest corner of the war. The fact that he immediately relinquished his son to my care told me how much he thought of me as a surgeon. As it was, his trust wasn't misplaced; the appendix I removed a short time later, enlarged with infection, could well have burst enroute to San Antonio.

I knew Colonel Hotchkiss, the commanding officer, would probably find out about the unauthorized procedure but I also felt I could handle whatever came of it, knowing I had probably saved the boy's life. From the beginning, the C.O. had little use for me, mainly because I'd been transferred there to replace his buddy, a doctor who was shipped out because of a serious drinking problem. I had no illusions about the Colonel's glee when he discovered my breach of protocol. I couldn't take time to speculate about my punishment, so I simply kept my mouth shut and hoped for the best. Not until close to the end of the war did I find out that the Colonel was aware of my insubordinate action and had signed orders for me to go to North Africa. The orders never made it through the rest of the chain of command because a particularly grateful sergeant and several of the enlisted men I'd treated waylaid them.

As the situation called for it, I waved a red cape at protocol many times after that, on duty and off. I think luck and good timing prevented me from receiving no worse than a "chewing out" from the C.O. over various matters. But I also believe that more often than not, someone I wasn't aware of at the time intervened on my behalf, usually because that person believed that what I was doing was right or had benefited from one of my actions. At least the restrictive life of medical school followed by four years in the army where someone was always looking over my shoulder tempered my actions to some extent. Whenever my actions provoked controversy, my friends—whether former patients, colleagues, or professionals who believed in my ability—backed me up.

If I'd had to worry about whether or not my actions could give a patient cause to bring a lawsuit against me, I don't know that I would have pursued private practice. For the first two decades of my practice, it never crossed my mind that a patient would sue me. After all, I wasn't making any money at two and three dollars an office visit. Whether the patient needed a C-section or removal of a mole, I never refused a service if the patient couldn't pay. Most people tried to pay, at a time when few even heard of insurance, much less could afford to buy any.

While returning to town one day from a housecall, a spontaneous stop at the residence of a patient gave me a perspective no insurance salesman or colleague could. The patient was a middle-aged woman I had seen for a condition that had progressed beyond effective treatment and convinced her to let me perform a hysterectomy within the next week. The woman's husband invited me to sit on the porch with him and as we rocked and talked, I tried to reassure him that the operation, though serious, would give his wife a quality of life she'd been deprived of for years because of a diseased reproductive system. A devout Christian, he believed that the outcome of major events in their lives, for good or bad, were "the Lord's will." Still, his response to my explanation for the surgery surprised me. "My wife thinks you're the best doctor she's ever been to," he said and as he paused, I'm sure my chest started to puff and head swell. "But I just want you to know one thing."

"What's that, Mr. Monroe?"

"If anything goes wrong and she doesn't make it, we won't hold it against you."

In hindsight, I think his religion made him a man at peace with the prospect of losing his wife. It didn't occur to me at that time, however. Being young and as hyperactive about my profession as a six-month-old Labrador Retriever on his first hunt, I convinced myself that the gleam in his eye was one of such confidence in my skill as a surgeon that nothing else needed to be said.

With great reluctance, I started carrying malpractice insurance in the seventies, mostly a result of wise counsel from Sarah and my colleagues. Even at that stage of my life, a certain naiveté clouded my judgment in treating patients. I didn't recognize that the dynamics of medical treatment were becoming extremely complex, especially with the growth of the insurance industry. This naiveté persisted in part because I avoided administrative and political arenas. If it was a choice between serving in a civic or medical organization and time I could spend with patients in the hospital or the office, I chose the latter every time.

One of the strongest criticisms I hear about the medical community today is the impersonal approach of physicians. In defense of their posture, I believe that a large part of the blame for this perception, whether true or not, is the fear of lawsuits. Another criticism is the exorbitant fees charged for so little time spent with the patient. Again, the dynamics of medicine, such as the overhead of employing a number of para-professionals to run the average office and conferencing needed to keep abreast of the latest changes in his own area of expertise, as well as the ever-expanding pharmaceutical industry, deserve as much of the blame for this perception. And I have not even mentioned the stranglehold that dealing with HMO's and Medicare documentation puts on the efficient billing and record-keeping in any office. If a doctor could simply be a doctor and worry less about being an administrator, politician, and, if billboards are any indication, a marketing executive, both patient and physician would benefit.

Though I envy young people in medicine today for their access to techniques and knowledge I didn't have, nothing could induce me to trade places with them. The price of their expertise is too costly; the kind of relationship I had with patients and the daily satisfaction of doing what I loved best defined a kind of practice that cannot exist in the present domicile of medicine.

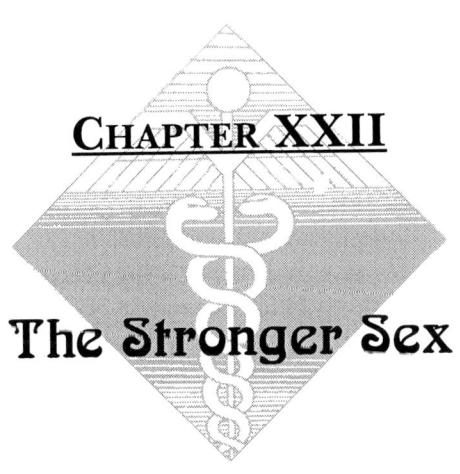

# Chapter XXII

# The Stronger Sex

I consider myself lucky, when it comes to the education I've received from women. Coming from the Victorian era, my mother raised her children with deference to rules of behavior that included manners in the home and in public that followed the strictest etiquette, or at least as much as a well-to-do family from a small town in north Texas knew about etiquette. Fifteen years his junior, Lee Ella Puckett so captivated my father upon their first meeting that he broke an engagement with another woman to court her. I never heard her address my father as anything other than "Mr. Taylor" and like the most proper matrons of her acquaintance, she insured that we attended church regularly. Though the era of her childhood discouraged spontaneous conduct or open displays of emotion, she had the common sense to allow her children a freedom of expression that many parents did not, including dancing lessons in our living room.

From the time I started to inch above my two older sisters in height, I was their dancing partner various and sundry afternoons after school. I rolled up the rug, Elleece cranked up the Victrola, and Elois practiced the latest steps of a waltz or polka with me, their shy, stuttering, red-headed "little" brother, Jimmie. I endured some pretty embarrassing moments, such as the time one of their friends dropped in while we were practicing and asked Elois if I had hair under my arms yet. The joy that dancing brought to me in later years however more than made up for my self-perceived martyrdom during that awkward time I bore the scrutiny of my sisters' girlfriends. I can thank my mother and sisters for helping me cross more than one cultural bridge.

By the time I had two years of medical school behind me and decided to specialize in gynecology, I suspected that the fairer sex was not the weaker sex. After treating women for problems ranging from hormone imbalance to endometriosis, delivering their children, and performing surgeries of utmost delicacy to their reproductive organs, I concluded that they were stronger than men in more ways than I'd ever imagined. I've known women who can juggle childrearing, housekeeping, and a job outside the home while undergoing sometimes enormous physical changes each month due to the menstrual cycle. As their physician, I've not only witnessed their ability to balance consistent discomfort and pain within their daily routine, but I've been privy to the very different paths they take mentally when under enormous stress. Women, whether family, friends, or patients, have taken me into their confidence because of my training. As a result of this association over these many decades, I stand in awe of the complex physiological and psychological processes that define them.

One of my more memorable instructors in medical school, a urologist named Al Folsum, used unusual analogies in class, particularly when he wanted to drive home a point about pathological studies of men and women. A short, stocky man with a booming voice, Dr. Folsum believed that a lecture or talk before any kind of group would fail without an introduction with a colorful anecdote, especially if the subject was dry or serious. In the speeches I've been asked to give over the years, I've subscribed faithfully to this approach, with varying degrees of success, if audience response is a measure.

But the most important insight I gleaned from Folsum's class was one that didn't fully impact me until many years later, when I realized it had more philosophical implications than practical. If I hadn't jumped from treating primarily men for nearly four years while in the service to a private practice that specialized in treating women, I probably wouldn't have given Folsum's lesson on similarities between male and female glandular tissue the consideration it deserved. Folsum dared us to discern the difference between a man's prostate tissue and a woman's breast tissue under a microscope. Expecting this to be an extension of his humorous way of making a point in lecture, we eagerly sought to prove him wrong. To our amazement, the structural parallelism between the samples made correct identification of the tissues a guessing game. As a student in medical school, this lesson competed with such a barrage of information I was expected to absorb daily that it failed to impress me as anything other than a simple lab exercise at the time. Only later reflection made me realize the lesson served as a reminder not to underestimate the complexity of nature, i.e. the underlying similarities between the male and female of the species.

During my internship at Parkland another incident significantly impacted my education about women. Just a week or two short of completing a year's work in pediatrics, a confrontation with a female physician put me at risk for losing the diploma recognizing that work.

My roommate, Bud, who had worked shifts with me at Bradford Memorial Hospital during most of that time, was with me the night we confronted the physician. We were scheduled to work that night but had asked this physician to cover our shift so that we could go to an annual dance for our class, commemorating the end of the school year. We never imagined that the physician would refuse to take our shift and like most of our peers, being young and cocksure, we had no backup plan. I didn't know how important the dance was to me until we literally had our coats over our arms and were heading for the exit of the hospital only to meet with adamant refusal from the physician to cover our shift. Even as I pointed out to her that we had worked long hours overtime for her and the hospital during the past year, I could tell by her air of condescension that she was going to be about as responsive to our plea as a sailboat in a hurricane.

The hospital administrator at Bradford Memorial, an RN named Burlew, was called in. She listened respectfully to both parties. Bud and I desperately needed the evening off, as much to relieve the tension as to meet socially with our classmates for what we knew might be the last time, due to many graduating and going into the service. The physician, an ascetic woman only a few years ahead of us in age but light years in maturity, stressed that she'd never been granted such a request from the doctors she worked under while a student. She didn't see why we should receive any special treatment.

Burlew's assessment was brief. "You'll have to stay," she announced to Bud and me. I made one more appeal to the physician, and the blow to my young ego when she again refused me in front of the administrator pushed me to say inwardly, 'The hell with the diploma,' while outwardly, I glanced at Bud, saw that he was with me on this, and told the two women that stood between us and the door that we were going.

A couple of weeks later, while on duty at Parkland's emergency room, the last thing on my mind was losing credit for the year of work I'd put in at Bradford Memorial. Since that time, Bud and I had separate assignments that kept us too busy to think about what we had given up for a good time with our classmates. I was taken completely by surprise when Burlew appeared on my shift and asked to speak to me. As we stepped into a quiet alcove, I thought she'd come to give me a lecture about responsibility. When she brought out my diploma she'd had tucked discreetly behind her back, my state of utter bafflement probably amused her, but she maintained the austerity for which she was reputed. Extending her other hand she said, "Doctor Taylor, I want to congratulate you on the fine job you did at Bradford Memorial."

Expecting to wake up from a dream, I accepted the diploma and shook her hand, the surprise rendering me speechless.

"I checked the records, talked to other physicians and nurses. You were right—Doctor Dryden and you deserved the time off that evening." I thanked her meekly, too stunned to fully appreciate her fairness in following up on the confrontation and tracking me down to give me the diploma.

The weaker sex? By the influx of females in traditionally male occupations the last half of this century, I'd speculate that most people find this phrase quaint, if not laughable. Perhaps the Sandra Day O'Connors and Jackie Joyner Kerseys of the next century will put this carryover from a less enlightened society to final rest.

# Epilogue

In the mid-eighties, a bad fall ended a physical regimen that began for me more than half a century earlier, but the mental adjustment I had to make in this phase of my life proved much more difficult than the physical.

If there was one habit I thought would be with me my entire life, it was doing pull-ups on a chinning bar. I grew up in an era when most boys my age idolized baseball players yet my most memorable role model was the itinerant boxer who boarded one winter with the family next door. Not only did he teach me about building upper body strength with daily workouts on a chinning bar, but he earned a following among several Cleburne lads with his tireless impromptu lessons in sparring and self-defense. Because of him, I learned to handle myself with my fists at an early age. This proved to be a mixed blessing; I never lacked for self-confidence when challenged by bigger or meaner boys but sometimes took unnecessary punishment because I relied on my physical ability to resolve a situation when I could have negotiated on less violent terms. Nevertheless, the lesson of the chinning bar stood me well in light of the pattern my life would take.

The unpredictability of housecalls and what I found in the way of assistance once I arrived at a patient's home dictated that a man in my profession had to be strong. Tending patients who weighed in excess of 200 pounds without an assistant with proper training or strength, or even worse, with distraught family members trying to help, made me a believer in my chinning bar exercises. Everywhere I've lived, from the basement of the fraternity house at medical school to my current residence, I didn't go a day without reps on the metal rod, usually mounted in a door frame. A stout back paid off on more than one occasion when I found myself digging the car out of a ditch after sliding off a rain-soaked county road. Likewise, the muscles I developed in my shoulders and forearms more than accommodated the strain of long and difficult surgeries.

Even after I sold my practice and accepted a lifestyle of semi-retirement, I still saw an occasional patient at my backdoor. Toward the end of 1987, I spent a great deal of time at Sarah's bedside, tending her in the terminal stage of occlusive arterial disease. One evening, my balance compromised by a combination of an encroaching sedentary lifestyle and the onset of heart disease, I slipped from a chair onto our hardwood floor at home. I knew as soon as I tried to get up I'd done more than bruise myself but I didn't want to alarm Sarah and went about my usual routine the rest of the evening, medicating myself for pain.

At first, I blamed the fall on simple fatigue. Within a few weeks, I sought the aid of the best facilities and physicians East Texas had to offer to diagnose what turned out to be a compression of the thoracic vertebra in my spine. The irreversible physical damage from that fall, which included a stooped posture that took several inches off my frame and reduced my breathing capacity, gave me reason to look deeper into the cause. My self-perceived invincibility so long ago initiated by the boxer's training, which sustained me through a lifestyle that involved daily assaults on my stamina and immune system, was in serious jeopardy. Suddenly I realized I was not only a septuagenarian, but as prone to the diminishing reflexes and increasing aches and pains as the next senior citizen. The aging process—a more insidious assailant to good health I've never met.

Within a few months, I lost Sarah. Up to that point, I thought I was adjusting to my physical setbacks as well as the next man, but with her passing and the resulting void in my life and in my house, the most vulnerable phase of my life was just beginning.

In 1992, my aortic valve faltered, throwing me into congestive heart failure. Meanwhile, I'd retired fully from medical practice and lapsed into a sedentary life. Coronary disease took its toll. As I entered Methodist Hospital in Houston in December of 1992 for a triple bypass and heart valve replacement, I didn't imagine that I was actually entering the happiest phase of my life.

My physical survival I owe to two extraordinarily-gifted physicians, Dr. Bill Henderson and Dr. Jimmy Howell. A true renaissance man in the field of medicine, Dr. Henderson holds a number of degrees and specialties, including internal medicine and cardiology. If not for his thorough approach to diagnostics and incredible instinct in assessing his patients, I probably would have failed to seek the surgery I needed in time to save my life. A physician who chose Nacogdoches for a practice when he could have gone anywhere, Dr. Henderson also follows a principle I've long believed in—when you've done as much as you can for the patient and he needs more specialized care, refer him to the best. By referring me to Dr. Howell for the cardiovascular surgery, Dr. Henderson did just that.

Jimmy Howell is a physician of mammoth talent. Considering the thousands of procedures he's performed in his career, the twelve-hour surgery that he and his team performed on me at Methodist Hospital three days after Christmas may have been typical for him, but for me, it was a miraculous extension of my life.

My mental outlook I owe to the woman who never left my side throughout the long ordeal of heart failure, surgery, and recovery. I can think of no better way to sum up Norma's effect on me than this: In the "third trimester" of my life, I am happier than I've ever been. In the wake of Sarah's death, Norma's compassion fortified me. During my convalescence after the heart surgery, her mental acuity and physical stamina awed me. Her beauty astounds me. I didn't think it could get much better when she became my wife in July of 1993. Yet her daily expressions of love sustain me beyond the bounds of the miraculous device implanted in me. Though we say "I love you" daily, sometimes it's simply the way she folds a napkin for me; other times it's the delight she shows when I call her to see a newcomer to the covey that accumulates at our patio bird feeders.

According to the 1999 *World Almanac,* heart disease is still the number one cause of death in this country. This came as no surprise to me but until I was the recipient of a survivor's award from the American Heart Association, I couldn't really appreciate what this meant from the patient's point of view. As a physician, I often took medical advances in stride, if not for granted. During the peak of my practice, I witnessed the advent of antibiotics, a polio vaccine, and heart transplants. But I couldn't truly appreciate the age of medicine we live in until I became a patient in need of a miracle. To the physicians who follow me, I hope you never take for granted the knowledge and tools at your disposal.

> Abou Ben Adhem (may his tribe increase!)
> Awoke one night from a deep dream of peace,
> And saw, within the moonlight in his room,
> Making it rich, and like a lily in bloom,
> An angel writing in a book of gold;
> Exceeding peace had made Ben Adhem bold,
> And to the presence in the room he said,
> 'What writest thou?'—The vision raised its head,
> And with a look made of all sweet accord,
> Answered 'The names of those who love the Lord.'
> "And is mine one?' said Abou. 'Nay, not so,'
> Replied the angel. Abou spoke more low,
> But cheerly still, and said, 'I pray thee then,
> Write me as one that loves his fellow-men.'
> The angel wrote, and vanished. The next night
> It came again with a great wakening light,
> And showed the names whom love of God had blessed,
> And lo! Ben Adhem's name led all the rest.

> Abou Ben Adhem and the Angel 1844
> —*The Poetical Works of Leigh Hunt*